# NORTHERN
# IRELAND

# NORTHERN IRELAND

## Time of Choice

**Richard Rose**

American Enterprise Institute for Public Policy Research
Washington, D. C.

Richard Rose is professor of politics at the University of Strathclyde, Glasgow, Scotland.

ISBN 0-8447-3206-0

Foreign Affairs Study 33, April 1976

Library of Congress Catalog Card No. 76-10080

*Printed in the United States of America*

To the people of

Antrim, Armagh, Down,
Fermanagh, Londonderry and Tyrone—
however they choose to describe themselves.


*They endured*

# ABBREVIATIONS

| | |
|---|---|
| B Specials | Ulster Special Constabulary (paramilitary police organization disbanded in 1969) |
| DUP | Democratic Unionist party (leader: Ian Paisley) |
| IRA | Irish Republican Army |
| IRSP | Irish Republican Socialist party |
| NILP | Northern Ireland Labour party |
| NIO | Northern Ireland Office of the United Kingdom government |
| PR | Proportional representation |
| RUC | Royal Ulster Constabulary (police force) |
| SDLP | Social Democratic and Labour party (leader: Gerry Fitt) |
| STV | Single transferable vote |
| UDA | Ulster Defence Association (Protestant paramilitary organization) |
| UDR | Ulster Defence Regiment (British army-led paramilitary reserve) |
| UPNI | Unionist party of Northern Ireland (leader: Brian Faulkner) |
| UUUC | United Ulster Unionist Council |
| UVF | Ulster Volunteer Force |
| UWC | Ulster Workers' Council |
| VUP | Vanguard Unionist party |

# CONTENTS

**LIST OF TABLES AND FIGURES**

## LIST OF MAPS

# BRITAIN AND IRELAND

ATLANTIC OCEAN

NORTH SEA

SCOTLAND

Glasgow

Edinburgh

NORTHERN
IRELAND

Belfast

Isle of
Man

REPUBLIC
OF IRELAND

Dublin

IRISH SEA

Manchester

Liverpool

Birmingham

WALES

ENGLAND

Cardiff

LONDON

ENGLISH CHANNEL

# INTRODUCTION

*For seven years the community has been torn and wounded by deep and unhappy differences. Our people have drained the cup of suffering. Some have been touched more closely and more poignantly than others, but no one has escaped, and no home and no family has been immune. The days of our affliction have been long.*

Opening statement of the chairman,
Northern Ireland Constitutional Convention,
8 May 1975

In most countries where they are held, elections decide who governs; in Northern Ireland, elections are about how the country should be governed—or whether it should be governed at all. For almost a century, a choice between alternative constitutions and national loyalties has been the central choice facing the voters of Northern Ireland. Elections have been concerned not so much with which party should govern Ulster, but rather with what country Northern Ireland belongs to, Great Britain or a united Ireland. Parties have disputed whether the electorate should be composed principally of Ulstermen, or citizens of the Republic of Ireland, or British voters, or some combination of these three groups. Lacking agreement about issues basic to governance, one or another (and sometimes several) of the major parties to the dispute have turned from election campaigns to military campaigns, hoping to decide with bullets what could not be decided with ballots.

Since 8 March 1973, the people of Northern Ireland have seven times gone to the polls to cast their votes—or to express their rejection of the system by spoiling their ballots. Ulstermen have been asked

1

to vote about everything from local government to the territorial sovereignty of the British Isles and the European Community. None of these elections has settled the problem of how Northern Ireland can be governed. On 1 May 1975, the people of Ulster were finally asked, for the first time in their history, to vote for representatives to a constitutional convention that would discuss new instruments of civil government. The initial reaction to the results—in London, in Dublin, and in many parts of Northern Ireland itself—was doubt about whether this ballot would be any more successful than its predecessors in bringing political stability to a much troubled land.

Politics aside—if that were possible—Northern Ireland might best be described as a small "nation" slightly outside the mainstream of Western industrial civilization. A visitor from London or New York enjoys the advantages of a small-scale society. A visitor from the coal fields of Pennsylvania or the English midlands marvels at the unspoiled landscape. Northern Ireland is less sunny but far greener than the Rocky Mountain states of America or the northern and western states of Australia. It is less isolated than Finland and less cursed with poverty than Southern Italy. All in all, a seasoned traveler would compare Northern Ireland with nearby parts of the British Isles—Wales and Scotland—and with the Republic of Ireland.

But politics can hardly be kept out of any study of life in Northern Ireland, past or present. The oldest vernacular epic in Western literature is an Ulster cycle of stories, the Tain, dating back to the sixth century A.D. It is a story of lust for power, as well as love; its pages are a chronicle of treachery, bloodshed, and death. Today the symbol of Ulster, derived from a Viking story, is a hand colored red by blood, and the songs that Belfast singers belt out to electric guitar accompaniment continue the woeful tale of Ulster's heroes—men who fight the British army or their fellow Ulstermen with high-powered Japanese-made rifles as well as with stones and cudgels. To them the red hand is the emblem of a nation yet to be.

Englishmen are tempted to dismiss Northern Ireland as Neville Chamberlain dismissed Czechoslovakia in 1938: "a far away country of whom we know nothing." Such an attitude betrays gross ignorance of the foundations of the United Kingdom and of its contemporary government. The religious conflict in Ulster today can be traced back to one of the great events in English history: the decision of King Henry VIII to break with the Roman Catholic Church in the sixteenth century. Queen Elizabeth II reigns today because of military victories that her Dutch Protestant forebear, William of Orange, won on Irish soil in the late seventeenth century. If Northern Ireland were dismissed from British sovereignty, the United Kingdom, a union of Great Britain and Northern Ireland, would no longer exist. Some Englishmen think it odd that many Ulstermen fervently protest their loyalty to the Crown that claims sovereignty over them, but their Ulster counterparts are equally puzzled that Englishmen, including high-ranking politicians, seem indifferent to the maintenance of the Crown's authority in the Irish part of what is meant to be a United Kingdom.

Those who call themselves Irishmen cannot be indifferent to the condition of Northern Ireland; it coexists on the same island with the Republic of Ireland. Prior to 1921, the whole island was under the British Crown. The nine counties of Ulster constituted one of the four historic provinces of the island. Today, the term Ulster is usually used to refer to six of these nine counties, the six that constitute the Northern Ireland portion of the United Kingdom. Three predominantly Catholic counties—Donegal, Cavan, and Monaghan—were assigned to the independent twenty-six-county Irish Free State (now the Republic of Ireland, or Eire) when it became independent in 1921.[1] The historic position of Ulster as part of Ireland was long accepted by Protestants as well as Catholics. Protestant Irishmen differed from Catholic Irishmen in regarding the *whole* of Ireland as best governed by union with Great Britain under the British Crown. Emigrant Irishmen, particularly those who value their ethnic traditions, may think of the six northeastern counties of Ireland as rightfully part of the Republic's territory. But when Irishmen who live in the Republic read about bombings and murders in the North, they become aware of the disadvantages of making the whole of Ireland one. To them it seems that violence might be the price of unity.

Americans should hesitate to distance themselves from Northern Ireland and its people, in view of the historic ties between the Province and the United States. Virginia on the east coast of America and Londonderry on Ulster's north coast were settled in the same year, 1607, as plantations chartered by the English Crown. Americans have inherited fewer problems from the past, but only because they were harsher in clearing their land of natives than were the English and Scots who came to Ireland in the century of Cromwell. In the eighteenth century, tens of thousands of Ulster Protestants emigrated to America in search of the religious freedom that was denied them

---

[1] In this study, the terms Northern Ireland, Ulster, and the Province are used interchangeably to refer to the six counties of Ireland under British sovereignty. The usage is adopted for the sake of simplicity, without political intent. Technically, no term suits exactly: for example, the northernmost part of the island lies in Donegal, a county of "southern" Ireland.

3

by an episcopal and established church. The descendants of these emigrants have provided America with eleven presidents. In the nineteenth century, Catholic Irishmen came in the hundreds of thousands, driven by famine and by the poverty of their condition. Their contribution to building America, in everything from the construction industry to modern political party organization, makes them equally prominent in American history.[2] Today Americans, Irish and otherwise, are as baffled by the conflict of Orange and Green as Ulstermen are by the conflict of black and white in the United States. By basing politics on religion rather than on race, Ulstermen are historically in the mainstream of European civilization.

Whatever their faith, the men and women of Ulster cannot afford to be indifferent to the condition of their land. It is where they live and where they expect to die. The recrudescence of the Troubles (a polite euphemism for the brutalities of internal war conducted by guerrilla units and the British army fighting an "alien" enemy) has brought premature death to more than 1,400 Ulster people, including children and adolescents. In this environment, the young mature quickly, for everyone is potentially a combatant or a victim. The political reawakening of Northern Ireland has had nightmarish qualities. A decade ago, Ulstermen witnessed violence at the cinema or in television news spots from Vietnam or from riot-torn American cities. Now they themselves are in the news, and the news is often bloody. While Ulster people may claim that they are not alone responsible for the depth of the Troubles, they have certainly done their share to create the political impasse of the present.

In his magisterial review of world history written more than a generation ago, Arnold J. Toynbee described industrial Ulster as "a social optimum between rural Scotland on the one hand and barbarian Appalachia on the other." In revising that study today, historians would draw different comparisons. Nonetheless, an English-speaking historian could not reject the basic assumption implicit in Toynbee's comparison: the people of Ulster are not a distant and alien lot, inconceivably remote from respectable people. Instead, they are part, albeit an often overlooked part, of the history of the English-speaking people. One does not need a surname such as Devlin, O'Neill, Cooper, Craig, or Hume to establish points of human or intellectual contact with the people of Ulster. Instead of passing judgment, the citizens

---

[2] See, for example, George W. Potter, *To The Golden Door: The Story of the Irish in Ireland and America* (Boston: Little, Brown, 1960); James G. Leyburn, *The Scotch-Irish: A Social History* (Chapel Hill: University of North Carolina Press, 1962); and E. R. R. Green, ed., *Essays in Scotch-Irish History* (London: Routledge, 1969).

of countries that have been historically linked with the Province might respond, thankfully and sympathetically: "There but for the grace of God go I."

The author of this monograph began studying Northern Ireland in 1965, a quiet time in the politics of the Province.[3] My chief motive was academic: to understand better the nature of political authority. There seemed little point in studying this question in England, where political authority was then unchallenged. Moreover, I was too far from my native America to follow properly the challenges to authority latent, or even realized, in the Deep South or in America's urban ghettos. Northern Ireland had a history of Protestant as well as Catholic challenges to political authority. In 1965 the Province was peaceful, yet its lawful government did not have the allegiance of all who were subject to its authority. My secondary motives for studying Ulster were practical: professional knowledge of British government, with which Northern Ireland invited comparison and contrast; easy access to the Province by boat or plane; and a knowledge of English, which, in a dry and witty dialect form, is the language of politics in Ulster. I had no personal or family attachments to Ireland, North or South.

Not for the first time in Irish history, life began to imitate art. A purely academic topic, political authority, was to become the central issue of Ulster politics from the launching of the civil rights campaign there in 1968 until now. The first fruits of my research were published as *Governing without Consensus: An Irish Perspective*.[4] That book was sent to the publishers in January 1971, shortly before the Troubles turned into something far worse, a type of war inaccurately but commonly called civil. I have continued my research into Northern Ireland politics since then, moved by sympathy with people whose lives are clouded by the terrible curse that history has laid upon them, by admiration for their courage and good humor in adversity, and by appreciation for their hospitality and courtesy to me through the years. I hope that Ulster readers may gain a little understanding from this volume, in return for what I have learned from them.

The gentle reader outside Northern Ireland, ensconced in comfortable liberal, conservative or, for that matter, Marxist assumptions about what makes the world go around, may find the subject of this book puzzling or disturbing in its juxtaposition of election results and

---

[3] For a factual and wide-ranging description of the society before the Troubles began again, see D. P. Barritt and C. F. Carter, *The Northern Ireland Problem* (London: Oxford University Press, 1962).

[4] Richard Rose, *Governing without Consensus: An Irish Perspective* (Boston: Beacon Press, and London: Faber, 1971).

accounts of death and destruction. Emotionally, one might prepare for a study of Ulster politics by reading the classics of tragedy, from Aeschylus's chronicle of the fall of the house of Atreus to William Faulkner's study of the Scotch-Irish settlers and ex-slaves of Mississippi and Sean O'Casey's plays about the nonheroic side of Dublin in 1916. A study of any century of European history, including the present war-torn century, might remind readers that the existence of a political problem is not proof that there is a solution.

This monograph is not intended to tell the reader everything that can be learned about politics—or life—from studying Ireland. To do that one would have to spend years reading the literature of a millenium collected in the great library of Trinity College, Dublin, as well as the ephemeral pamphlets of the Troubles since 1968 held in the Linenhall Library, Belfast. The object of this study is to set out the dominant features of Northern Ireland politics today and the choices ahead for the disputed government of the Province. The election on 1 May 1975 of the Northern Ireland Constitutional Convention focused and magnified the significance of these choices for the future. It is important for Ulstermen and for influential persons elsewhere to understand both their nature and their consequences.

In preparing this study, I have drawn upon many conversations held over the years with people who are or have been intimately involved in Northern Ireland affairs. In the nature of things, the help of such individuals must be anonymous. I would like to thank publicly two graduate students at the University of Strathclyde, Ian McAllister and Sarah Nelson, for their comments upon this manuscript and to thank Ian McAllister for doing the tedious calculations required in the election analysis in Chapter 5. The publishers are also to be thanked for doing their best to bring out so quickly a study that, it is hoped, has both topical and durable value. The author alone is responsible for any errors of fact as well as for the interpretation contained herein.

# 1

# THE PROBLEM BRIEFLY STATED

*I know very well that the motto of every government—*
*it is pasted outside every department—is "Peace in our time,*
*O Lord." But you do not get rid of the difficulty—be it*
*today or tomorrow or a year hence, or be it six years hence.*
*The difficulty will remain, and Ulster will be a physical and*
*geographical fact.*

Sir Edward Carson, 1914

Northern Ireland is the point at which the two islands of Ireland and Great Britain meet. Physically, Ulster is a part of the island of Ireland. Until a century ago, however, approach by water was far easier than approach by land. Ulster's propinquity by water to northern England and Scotland—only twelve miles distant at the narrowest point of the Irish sea—resulted in continual movement back and forth between Britain and the northeast of Ireland, much more than between Ulster and the less accessible counties of Ireland's other provinces. In area, Northern Ireland covers 5,452 square miles. It is about the size of the southeast of England, slightly larger than the state of Connecticut or than Flanders or Wallonia, the two constituent parts of Belgium.

Northern Ireland's population was reported as 1,536,000 in the 1971 census. One-third of its people live in and around Belfast, the industrial and commercial as well as political capital of the Province. Londonderry, its second city, has a population of only 52,000. Belfast grew up in the late eighteenth century, one of the first cities affected by the Industrial Revolution. Shipbuilding and textiles were among its early industries. Today it builds supertankers and aircraft and provides services for synthetic textile factories scattered along the Antrim coast. Yet within an hour or two's drive from the city, a rural

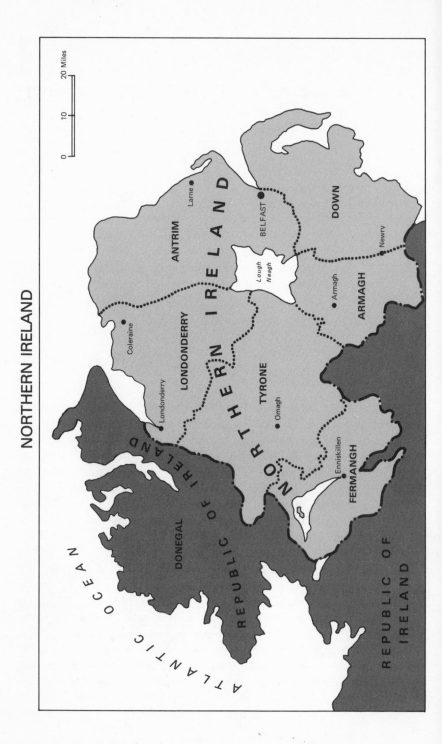

NORTHERN IRELAND

ATLANTIC OCEAN

REPUBLIC OF IRELAND

DONEGAL

REPUBLIC OF IRELAND

NORTHERN IRELAND

ANTRIM

Larne

BELFAST

DOWN

Newry

Lough Neagh

Armagh

ARMAGH

LONDONDERRY

Coleraine

Londonderry

TYRONE

Omagh

FERMANGH

Enniskillen

0   10   20 Miles

way of life has survived that reflects the era before the Industrial Revolution. The hill farmers of Fermanagh and Tyrone live in the penumbra of a still older Celtic world. The standard of living, as measured in gross national product per capita, is less than that of England but higher than that of the Republic of Ireland. Those who live there value Ulster as their home. Those who put money first follow generations of their kinsmen and emigrate to England, America, or places further afield.

Northern Ireland is neither a nation nor a state. In law, it is a subordinate part of the United Kingdom, ruled by the authority of the British Parliament at Westminster. In fact, Northern Ireland is an insubordinate part of the United Kingdom—governed without consensus when it is governed at all. That is the Northern Ireland problem.

Ireland's past is very nearly its present; the Troubles of the past keep recurring. The Protestant wall slogan is, "Remember 1690." Praising a land that was Gaelic, Catholic, and free, Catholic Irishmen invoke a period that elsewhere in Europe was known as the Dark Ages. Three themes are of enduring significance in Irish history. The first is that the people of the island have never shared a single national identity; the second, that religion has divided rather than united the people of Ireland; the third, that there has never been a time when all the people of Ireland have been effectively governed by an authority they fully accepted as legitimate.

## Nationality

The peoples of Ireland are descended from successive waves of immigrants and invaders. The Celts became established in Ireland about two centuries before the birth of Christ.[1] They came in small bands and not, as the Romans came to Britain, with an army organized to establish a settled political authority. Invading Norsemen founded Dublin in the middle of the ninth century. The Norman conquest of England in 1066 was followed in 1169 by an Anglo-Norman conquest of Ireland—or as one scholar phrases it, "the half-conquest," for the island was divided between the "old" or "mere" Irish and those who

---

[1] For historical details of the movement of peoples in and out of Ireland, see J. Raftery, ed., *The Celts* (Cork: Mercier Press, 1964) and M. W. Heslinga, *The Irish Border as a Cultural Divide* (Assen, the Netherlands: Van Gorcum, 1962). One Irish scholar, Liam de Paor, has argued that the Celts might better be described as the Megalithic people because of their distinctive use of stones. See "Celts, Saints, and Menhirs," *Irish Times* (Dublin), 15 April 1975.

took up the habits and outlook of their Anglo-Norman governors.[2] The English victory in the sixteenth-century religious wars in Ireland was followed by the arrival of English and Scots settlers in Ulster starting in 1607.

Soon after the American Revolution, Irishmen took up arms in defense of what they regarded as inalienable rights. In 1798 a group calling itself the United Irishmen rebelled against the British Crown, seeking the same independence that the Americans had recently won. They failed. Throughout the nineteenth century, Irish politicians increasingly sought a distinctive form of government for Ireland on the grounds that the Irish people, like the Italians or the German nation, had a right to its own state. The claim was given half-hearted recognition in the British Parliament's proposals for some form of devolved home rule, but these proposals were never implemented as intended. In 1916 a small group of rebels entered the Dublin General Post Office and proclaimed an Irish Republic. Ulster was assumed to be part of their rebel state. The leaders of the Easter rising, as it came to be known, were executed by the British, but many of their hopes were realized in the creation of a twenty-six-county Irish Free State in 1921. Six counties of Ulster remained within the United Kingdom, because the Protestants who predominated there were just as ready and successful as the rebellious Republicans in the south in fighting for their cause, namely, to remain under the British Crown.

In Northern Ireland today everyone has a sense of national identity, but there is no agreement about the nation to which the people of Ulster belong. Three-quarters of the Catholics think of themselves as Irishmen, according to a survey of Ulster loyalties conducted shortly before the outbreak of the present Troubles,[3] but only 15 percent identify with Britain, their nation according to United Kingdom law. Protestants disagree among themselves. The largest single fraction (39 percent) choose British identity, but others identify first with Ulster or with Ireland. Protestants are less sure of their national identity than are Catholics. The bulk of Catholics regard themselves as Irish because Ireland is where they have been born and bred, a fact that no government can change. By contrast, Protestants who identify with Britain believe that they are British because they are governed under the British Crown—an authority that many Irishmen wish to repudiate.

---

[2] See F. X. Martin, "The Anglo-Norman Invasion," in T. W. Moody and F. X. Martin, eds., *The Course of Irish History* (Cork: Mercier Press, 1967), pp. 142-43.
[3] For full details of Ulster attitudes toward national identity, see Rose, *Governing without Consensus*, Chapter 6.

In aggregate, Irish identity is mentioned most often, but it is the choice of a minority (43 percent) of Ulstermen. By contrast, 29 percent think of themselves as British and 21 percent identify first of all with Ulster. The fact that the people of Northern Ireland disagree about their national identity is reflected in politics. Within a few square miles of Belfast, four different flags can be seen symbolizing different loyalties: the British Union Jack, which is the official emblem of the state; the Irish tricolor, the flag of the Dublin-based Irish Republic; the red hand of Ulster, symbol of a nascent Ulster nationalism found primarily among Protestants; and the Plough and the Stars, the emblem of James Connolly, a leader of the 1916 Dublin rising, sometimes flown by a small group of socialist Republicans.

## Religion

Religion has been central to political conflict in Ireland since the Reformation in the sixteenth century. Henry VIII, king of Ireland as well as England, established a Church of Ireland subject to his own political authority along with the Church of England. Henry expected his loyal Irish subjects to become Protestants, as the great bulk of his English subjects did. This was not to be. Most Irishmen remained loyal to the Pope and thus disloyal to the Crown. They showed their disloyalty by joining in a series of European wars, from the mid-sixteenth to the end of the seventeenth century, with the intention of reestablishing a Catholic sovereign in both England and Ireland.

Religious identification thus came to determine political loyalties in Ireland—a pattern that has persisted with varying intensity ever since. For century after century, Catholics, sometimes organizing along sectarian lines and sometimes on a secular basis, with support from small numbers of Protestants, have asserted a claim to Irish national independence. This has been opposed by the forces of the Protestant British Crown. The measures taken to repress Irish rebellion tended to identify the Catholic Church closely with those who saw themselves as Irishmen, thus preventing the growth of anticlerical or secular thought. Among Protestants, those who have lapsed from the fundamentalist tenets of their Reformation faith have not embraced the theology of a Counter-Reformation Irish Catholic Church. Nor have they wished to exchange government by a conventionally "liberal" Britain for government from Dublin, where church and state are closely linked in many ways.

If religion is measured by church attendance, Northern Ireland is probably the most Christian society in the Western world except for the Republic of Ireland. Among Protestants, 46 percent report attending church at least once a week, and another 18 percent at least monthly; this is up to four times the figure for church attendance in such Protestant countries as England or Sweden. Among Catholics, 33 percent go to church more than once a week, and another 62 percent report weekly attendance; this is two to three times higher than the rates of church attendance in such nominally Catholic countries as France, Italy, or Austria. Protestants and Catholics agree about the importance of religious beliefs, and they believe in a fundamentalist interpretation of the Bible. While fundamentalism makes adherents of both religions believe in the Devil, denominational differences lead Ulstermen to disagree about which church is the spokesman for the Antichrist in Northern Ireland today.

Contrary to what sociologists assume, religious differences do not correlate strongly with social differences in Northern Ireland. The bulk of the poor people, like the bulk of the well-to-do in Ulster, are Protestant—because Protestants constitute two-thirds of the population. Catholics tend to be disproportionately numerous in the less advantaged groups in society, but the differences are of a few percentage points. There are well-to-do Catholics and poor Catholics. There are not caste differences of the kind that existed in parts of the old American South or in the African colonies of the British Empire. Class differences are less noticeable in Ulster than in London. Moreover, class identification is weak: only 12 percent of Ulstermen identify strongly with a social class, while 38 percent have a strong sense of national identity and 42 percent identify strongly with their religion.[4]

While Ulster people have a fierce loyalty to place, identifying with the county and the townland in which they live as well as with their nation, the primary identification of political significance today remains religion. Ulstermen speak of two communities, Protestant and Catholic, even within a village of 100 or 200 people. A nearly complete segregation of schooling by religion makes it possible to ascertain a stranger's religion by asking what school he went to—as well as by observing the various subtle distinctions that Ulstermen detect between "Protestant" and "Catholic" behavior. For decades, the population of Northern Ireland has been two-thirds Protestant and one-third Catholic. The 1971 census found 65.3 percent reporting membership in more than sixty different Protestant denominations (of

---

[4] For comparative data of the socioeconomic conditions of American Southerners and Ulstermen, see Donald Matthews and J. W. Prothro, *Negroes and the New Southern Politics* (New York: Harcourt, Brace, 1966) and Rose, *Governing without Consensus*, Chapters 9-10.

which the Presbyterian Church and the Episcopal Church of Ireland together account for four-fifths); 34.7 percent describe themselves as Roman Catholics.[5]

Throughout this book, individuals, groups, and organizations will be referred to as Protestant or Catholic because that is the way that Ulster people speak and think about themselves. A local story has it that anyone who claims to be an atheist must say whether he is a Protestant atheist or a Catholic atheist. To be neither one thing nor the other is almost as difficult in Northern Ireland as to be neither black nor white in the American Deep South. Organizations can be classified by religion, because their membership is exclusively or overwhelmingly Protestant (Orange) or Catholic (Green) in a society where this fact has major political implications.[6] The use of religious labels in no way implies that religious hierarchies or synods formally endorse the organizations or groups so described. On the other hand, clergymen are also Ulstermen—and they usually share with their fellow citizens political views appropriate to the community to which they belong.

Political parties, too, are clearly identified with the religious communities. Until the 1970s, the dominant Unionist party normally chose members of the exclusively Protestant Orange Order as its candidates for Parliament. The chief opposition group, the Nationalists, was based on parochial as well as constituency organization; priests often chaired political meetings, and Nationalist candidates were invariably Catholic. Only 5 percent of Catholics voted for the perennially victorious Unionist party, and less than 1 percent of Protestants for the chief alternative, the Nationalist party.

Religion, national identity, and political loyalty—precisely the matters about which Ulstermen disagree—have been the dominant causes of war and political disruption in Europe for centuries. Conflict about the nature of the state is endemic in Ulster politics because the groups involved define the basic problem in different and unrelated terms. Catholics usually see the problem in terms of nationality; an appropriate solution, they think, is the abolition of the border with

---

[5] Because of the Troubles in 1971 some census forms were not completed and no religion was stated in 9.4 percent of census returns. The proportions of Protestants and Catholics are calculated from the 90.6 percent stating their religion in the census. For a case study of a village, see Rosemary Harris, *Prejudice and Tolerance in Ulster: A Study of Neighbours and "Strangers" in a Border Community* (Manchester: Manchester University Press, 1972).

[6] In Northern Ireland, the symbolic colors are orange for the Protestants, after King William of Orange, the Dutch general who put down a seventeenth-century Catholic rebellion, and green for Catholics, a color traditionally associated with Ireland.

the Republic of Ireland and the creation of a thirty-two-county Republic. This view is endorsed by the constitution of the Irish Republic. It is also endorsed by recurring British references to the importance of an ill-defined "Irish dimension" in the politics of the most "alien" part of the United Kingdom. Protestants have tended to see the conflict in religious terms, regarding Catholics as disloyal to the British Crown because they wish to establish a thirty-two-county Irish Republic in which Catholics would form more than three-quarters of the population. The Protestants complain that home rule for Ireland is "Rome rule"; and indeed, the legislation of the Irish Republic more faithfully mirrors Catholic doctrines—in its nonrecognition of divorce and contraception, for example—than that of any other European country.[7] Within Ulster, Protestants pointedly blame the problems of the Province on the disloyalty of the Republicans, who are invariably Catholic, and on the violence of the clandestine Irish Republican Army (IRA), which has its base of support within the Catholic community. By its own standards, each side is right, and uncompromisingly so.

## Government without Consensus

These conflicts about ends are used to justify many means of conflict. Because each side believes it is right, it believes it may use "all means which may be found necessary" to achieve its goal, as the 1912 Ulster Protestant Covenant put it. The "fundamental right" of nationhood may be "asserted in arms," said the proclamation of the Easter 1916 Republican rebellion in Dublin. It is debatable whether electoral politics or the politics of coercion has been more "normal" in Ireland. Centuries of internal disorder, conquest, and insurrection have made Ulster politicians view as normal many tactics that elsewhere might be thought to violate both the spirit and the letter of the law. In a land where rebellion is traditional and rebels are armed, a prudent political movement looks to its strength in arms, as well as to its electoral strength.

Until the establishment of a southern and a northern Irish government, the British alternated between conciliation and coercion in their treatment of Ireland. Both policies failed. The founders of the new Irish Free State, having won independence for a twenty-six-county state through a rebellion, promptly found themselves faced

---

[7] For a dispassionate and scholarly account of the role of the Catholic Church in the Republic, see John H. Whyte, *Church and State in Modern Ireland, 1923-1970* (Dublin: Gill & Macmillan, 1971).

14

with a split in the Republican movement. They had failed to wrest a republic of thirty-two counties from the Crown. The disagreement between those Republicans who were determined to fight for this end and those who were prepared to settle for the Free State was ended in 1923 by a civil war that was unusually bloody even by Irish standards. The Irish Republican Army remained in being, however, as an illegal underground force to fight against the regimes in both Dublin and Belfast and for the creation of a thirty-two-county Ireland. In Northern Ireland Protestants secured their position within the United Kingdom by establishing a home guard military force to defeat Republican rebels there. Belfast itself was under curfew for more than a year. From the mid-1920s the Parliament of Northern Ireland established at Stormont ruled with little violence, for the defeated Catholics did not wish to challenge a police force and a paramilitary service that were ready to die or kill to maintain their constitution. Protestants had no wish to resort to violence, for their dominant numbers ensured that each election would return a party pledged, in the words of one prime minister, to maintain "a Protestant Parliament for a Protestant people." [8]

While no society receives the full allegiance of 100 percent of its citizens, Englishmen (except in Ireland) expect that the overwhelming mass of the population will be fully allegiant, supporting the institutions of political authority and complying with basic political laws.[9] Americans share the expectation of governing with consensus. Individuals and parties disagree about particular policies, but virtually everyone agrees about the regime that should take decisions and will comply with the decisions of the legitimate government.

Northern Ireland has always been governed without consensus. Less than half the population has been *fully allegiant,* that is, prepared to support the constitutional government of the day and to comply with its basic laws.[10] More than one-third are *ultra-loyal,* that is, they support authority—but will only conditionally comply with laws. They reserve the right to defy any law that they regard as interfering with their self-defined rights (for example, a British act of Parliament requiring cooperation with the Republic of Ireland) and even to over-

---

[8] Lord Craigavon's statement of 1937 is quoted from Barritt and Carter, *The Northern Ireland Problem,* p. 46. See also Eamon de Valera's description of Ireland as a "Catholic nation," as found in Rose, *Governing without Consensus,* p. 247.

[9] For an extensive discussion of different types of political authority, see Richard Rose, "Dynamic Tendencies in the Authority of Regimes," *World Politics,* vol. 21, no. 4 (1969).

[10] See Rose, *Governing without Consensus,* Chapter 5.

throw a constitutionally determined government. A third and smaller group is *disaffected:* they do not support the political authority of the day, but are prepared to comply with its laws for pragmatic reasons. A disaffected subject, like a fully allegiant citizen, obeys laws, but he would welcome the overthrow of the government making them. Disaffected subjects are "neutral against" authority. Those who reject political authority and refuse to comply with its laws are *rebels.* While numerically few, rebels have a political importance out of all proportion to their numbers—and they figure prominently in the pantheon of Ulster's political heroes.

To govern without consensus is to accept rebels and disaffected citizens as facts of life. Rather than giving first priority to winning the allegiance of the groups that are opposed in principle to established authority, those in power may give first priority to maintaining a preponderant majority in support of the regime as it exists, warts and all. In the absence of consensus, any government can take comfort in the fact that it has friends as well as enemies. To seek friends among one's enemies is to risk making enemies of one's friends. Efforts at conciliation may lead to the downfall of an established regime—rather than to the consensus that is, in the long run, the theoretical ideal.

The dominant coalition in Ulster politics from the 1920s to the late 1960s was a coalition of fully allegiant and ultra-loyal citizens. Both supported government through the institutions of a Northern Ireland Parliament. The two groups differed insofar as the "ultras" were so loyal to principles of Protestant rule that they would not allow any act of the British Parliament to challenge this, whereas fully allegiant Ulstermen accepted the ultimate sovereignty of the British government. The bulk of Catholics were disaffected: they complied with the law, but did not support the constitution. Only a small proportion allied themselves with the rebellious campaigns of the Irish Republican Army; they reckoned that rebellion would lead to a bloody civil war in which the Catholics would be defeated. The coalition fell apart in the late 1960s, when Terence O'Neill, the Unionist prime minister, sought to win full allegiance from the Catholics and succeeded only in inciting a backlash from the ultra-loyalists. Concurrently, Catholic disaffection expressed itself in a new form— illegal but nonviolent protest—and latterly in armed rebellion.

While the causes of political discord within Northern Ireland tend to be constant from generation to generation, the outcome of any given crisis is not predictable, for the numerous groups involved can combine in many different ways. The purpose of this study is to analyze the choices about future government facing the people of Northern Ireland today. To do this, one must first review the events that have brought the people of Northern Ireland to the political precipice where they now stand and consider the parties to the dispute, both electoral and armed. The election of the Northern Ireland Constitutional Convention in May 1975 focused the attention of Ulster people upon deciding what instruments of government they—rather than Dublin or London—wished to prevail. Analysis of party programs and of voting patterns shows to what extent individual choices have led to collective deadlock. Anyone reviewing the various prospects for governing without consensus in Northern Ireland today may think all of them unattractive, but the alternative to governing without consensus is not necessarily governing with consensus. Instead it may be disorder and anarchy on a scale unknown anywhere in the Western world since the final months of the Second World War.

# 2
# TO THE PRECIPICE

*Take away this murdering hate.*

Sean O'Casey, *Juno and the Paycock*

The political traditions of Northern Ireland constitute a mixed inheritance. Some of their features have enabled Northern Ireland to be governed peacefully for much of its history; others have led to intermittent violence and rebellion, bringing the Province to the precipice of political destruction today.

## Stormont, 1921–1972

From 1921 until 1972, the power for governing Northern Ireland was primarily vested in a Northern Ireland prime minister and cabinet, responsible to a locally elected Parliament of Northern Ireland which sat at Stormont, a park-like estate outside Belfast.[1] The British government at Westminster reserved to itself control of foreign policy and defense, as well as the regulation of taxation and revenue. But these powers—elsewhere considered of prime importance—were of less interest to Ulstermen than the powers given to Stormont to maintain the security of the Province through locally controlled police, courts, and uniformed paramilitary auxiliaries. Ulstermen were more concerned with protecting themselves from civil war than with prepar-

---

[1] For a description of the institutions of government under Stormont, see Nicholas Mansergh, *The Government of Northern Ireland* (London: Allen & Unwin, 1936); T. Wilson, ed., *Ulster under Home Rule* (London: Oxford University Press, 1955); and R. J. Lawrence, *The Government of Northern Ireland: Public Finance and Public Services, 1921-1964* (Oxford: Clarendon Press, 1965).

ing to ward off a Russian or German attack. The British government was happy to accept this arrangement, for it freed Westminster from responsibility for dealing with the sort of eruptions of Irish violence that had distracted the British House of Commons from the 1880s to 1921. Benign neglect was the British policy toward Ulster. Until 1968, not a single civil servant in Whitehall was concerned full-time with the politics of the Province.

The institutions of government at Stormont were, like many things in Dublin, modelled on British counterparts familiar to everyone in the Anglo-American world. Whatever their political differences, Ulstermen agree about one thing: the positive value of freely elected representative government. They disagree about whether the government should represent a British or an Irish people.

Ulster Protestants have supported government by an elected majority because they have always constituted two-thirds of the electorate in Northern Ireland: as long as Protestants are united politically, they can be sure of determining the outcome of every election, just as Catholics can in the Republic or white voters in a gubernatorial election in Alabama or Mississippi. For nearly half a century, Protestants supported Unionist party candidates pledged to maintain the union with Britain and opposed any measures encouraging the growth of Republican or Catholic influence (the two terms are often used interchangeably) in Northern Ireland. At the first election held in 1921, Unionists won 66.9 percent of the vote; at the final Stormont election held in 1969, official and unofficial Unionists won 67.4 percent of the vote. In a Parliament with fifty-two members, the Unionists usually won about three-quarters of the seats, and their strength never fell below 65 percent in the Stormont House of Commons. In a phrase used of post-Civil War America, Ulstermen were ready to vote as they shot; only one contested constituency ever swung between the predominantly Protestant Unionist party and the predominantly Catholic Nationalists.[2]

Catholics tended to ignore Stormont election results, leaving a majority of seats uncontested, because they considered the creation of a predominantly Protestant six-county Northern Ireland an illegitimate gerrymander. They thought Ulstermen should vote in an all-Ireland election along with the Irishmen of the twenty-six counties.

[2] Dock, Belfast, was the marginal constituency; three other constituencies changed hands across the Unionist/Nationalist divide—but only because of abstentionist policies among Republicans, or two candidates' splitting one community's vote. For a definitive record of Stormont election results, see Sydney Elliott, *Northern Ireland Parliamentary Election Results, 1921-1972* (Chichester, Sussex: Political Reference Publications, 1973).

In such an electorate Unionists would be a permanent minority: 1,250,000 Protestants compared with about 3,250,000 Catholics. Ulster Unionists emphasized that the partition of Ireland would never have come about had southern Irishmen not rebelled against the old United Kingdom. In a United Kingdom of Great Britain and the whole of Ireland, Irish Protestant and British voters would outnumber Catholic Irishmen by a margin of more than ten to one.

**The Revival of the Troubles.** The Catholics' rejection of the Stormont regime took three forms. In the first place, the Nationalist party, representing the bulk of Catholics, refused to accept the title of loyal opposition. It proclaimed it was *not* loyal to the United Kingdom of which Stormont was a part; it desired instead a united Ireland. Second, some Ulster Catholics asserted their Irishness in ways that simultaneously fulfilled their pride and inflamed Protestant opinion: by holding parades commemorating the Dublin Easter rising against the British, for example, or displaying the Irish tricolor, an illegal emblem according to an act of the Stormont Parliament. Even sports were not immune. Catholics tended to play distinctively Irish games organized by the Gaelic Athletic Association, linked with the Republican movement. Third, a few Catholics resorted to bloody street fighting.

The Stormont system persisted for two generations with little significant challenge, because Ulstermen did not wish to return to the violence of the early 1920s. Belfast had been the scene of periodic and bloody rioting in the generations leading up to and after the First World War. In the Troubles of the early 1920s, 544 people died. From the mid-1920s settlement to the recurrence of the Troubles in the late 1960s, the Province was relatively peaceful. In politically significant riots in 1932, two men died, and in 1935 about a dozen. In the IRA campaign in Ulster from 1956 to 1962, the total number of deaths was eighteen.

The Unionist monopoly of power at Stormont crumbled during the prime ministership of Captain Terence O'Neill, who took office in 1963. O'Neill's aim was novel, even revolutionary: he sought nothing less than a fully legitimate regime supported by a consensus of Catholics as well as Protestants. O'Neill believed that economic growth could provide the means for diverting Catholics from "old-fashioned" aspirations to Irish unity and for assuaging Protestant fears of Catholic competition for jobs. He also sought friendlier relations with the Republic; his meeting with its prime minister, Sean Lemass, a veteran of the 1916 rebellion, was comparable to a summit meeting between

Eisenhower and Khrushchev in the era of the cold war. Within Ulster, O'Neill encouraged toleration of the Catholic minority.[3]

While O'Neill's policies were welcomed by liberal Protestants, a small group in a divided society, they smacked of treason to ultra-loyal Protestants. In 1964 the Rev. Dr. Ian Paisley, a Free Presbyterian minister, first became politically prominent when he led street demonstrations against the display of an Irish tricolor in Belfast. Subsequent demonstrations twice earned Paisley three-month jail sentences. By 1970 they had gained him sufficient popular support to win his election to a Northern Ireland seat at the Westminster Parliament—with Terence O'Neill, by now retired from public life, one of his constituents.

Initially Catholic leaders gave tacit support to the bridge-building efforts of the Unionist government. But the two ends never met. Nationalists hesitated to support policies that might give Catholic votes to the Unionist party. Republicans were not interested in improving their lot within Ulster; instead, they wished to abolish the border that separated them from the twenty-six counties. Catholics of all political outlooks waited and waited in vain for the "new" Unionist government to give them political influence, as well as tokens of toleration. By the summer of 1968, younger Catholics had given up hope of meaningful change. Inspired in part by the civil rights movement in America, Catholic activists took to the streets in massive protest marches.[4] Their demonstrations were sometimes conducted in violation of Stormont laws and regulations, which put them outside the scope of political change by the ballot. But they were also peaceful, unlike the illegal bombings and shootings that characterized the IRA campaigns against Stormont. Moreover, the civil rights groups of Northern Ireland were not demanding Irish unity, but rather better houses, jobs, the repeal of a special powers act violating the European Convention on Human Rights, and, most of all, "one man, one vote, one value."

The civil rights campaign brought Northern Ireland to the attention of the world when demonstrators were fiercely clubbed down by the Royal Ulster Constabulary (RUC) at a demonstration in Londonderry on 5 October 1968. The Stormont government remained in office but it was pressed by London to make concessions to the

---

[3] For O'Neill's account of his term of office, see his collected speeches, *Ulster at the Crossroads* (London: Faber, 1969) and *The Autobiography of Terence O'Neill* (London: Rupert Hart-Davis, 1972).

[4] For a detailed comparison, see Richard Rose, "On the Priorities of Citizenship in the Deep South and Northern Ireland," *Journal of Politics*, forthcoming, 1976.

Catholics in the hope that this would secure more consent for the government. The concessions were few—but numerous enough to fan Protestant suspicions of a sellout to Dublin. Terence O'Neill failed in an appeal for popular endorsement in a snap election in February 1969 and shortly thereafter resigned from office. His successor, Major James Chichester-Clark, lasted until March 1971, when he too fell because of a loss of confidence among ultra-loyalists. The British government gave Stormont money to expand housing and employment programs. But political change was slow to come. Instead of allowing Catholics a share in power, the reforms neutralized government by taking power from the Unionists and placing it in the hands of professional experts.

On 12 August 1969, Protestant groups marched in Londonderry to commemorate the 280th anniversary of the relief of the Protestant community that was besieged there in 1689 by a Catholic army intent upon reclaiming the whole of Ireland for enemies of the English Crown. During the day, stone throwing broke out between Protestant and Catholic groups, escalating to a full-fledged "rising" in the Bogside, the Catholic quarter outside the walls where the Catholic siege army had once camped. Disorder followed in Belfast and several other towns, and the indigenous police and paramilitary reserves were unable to contain it. Eight civilians died in the events of the week. British troops were introduced to restore public order amidst the Troubles.[5]

The inability of the Royal Ulster Constabulary to maintain order led both Catholics and Protestants to arm themselves, for fear that the British army would not be around forever to protect them from their traditional enemy. Protestants showed their firepower first in shootings directed at the RUC and British soldiers in October 1969. But the British army more often searched for arms in Catholic areas. In the first weekend of July 1970, it placed 20,000 Catholics in the Lower Falls area of Belfast under around-the-clock curfew when a successful arms raid met with armed resistance by the IRA. After unsuccessful and unpublicized efforts to avoid a recurrence, a "shooting war" between the IRA and the British army broke out in February 1971.

---

[5] The events of 1968-69 are reviewed by The Cameron Commission, *Disturbances in Northern Ireland* (Belfast: Her Majesty's Stationery Office, Cmnd. 532, 1969). For a detailed chronology of the Troubles, see Richard Deutsch and Vivien Magowan, *Northern Ireland, 1968-73: A Chronology of Events*, vol. 1, 1968-71; vol. 2, 1972-73; vol. 3, 1974 (Belfast: Blackstaff Press). See also the files of *Fortnight*, an independent Belfast political journal published since 1970.

**Violence and Internment Again.** The introduction of internment without trial on 9 August 1971 was an admission that the disturbed situation was beyond the bounds of customary British government procedures.[6] On that day the British army provided the force to intern more than 300 Catholics who allegedly threatened the security of the Stormont regime. Internment had proven effective in reducing challenges to public order during disturbances in the early 1920s and during the 1956–1962 IRA campaign. But this time the result was different. The Catholic community regarded the internees not as terrorists, but as victims of actions by an illegitimate regime. Instead of supporting the lawful, albeit exceptional, acts of government or remaining sullenly but passively disaffected, Catholics of all political persuasions or none joined together to resist internment and the police and military actions taken to arrest and screen tens of thousands of Catholic suspects. The introduction of internment of Protestants on 5 February 1973, albeit on a much smaller scale, did not assuage the anger of the minority community. A total of 2,158 orders leading to internment were issued from 9 August 1971 to 10 February 1975, at which point, following the announcement of an IRA truce, the British government suspended its policy of holding people indefinitely without charge and trial and began the gradual and systematic release of internees, letting the last group out of custody on 5 December 1975. The end of internment was justified on the grounds that it had not proven an effective means of combatting continuing violence.

The aftermath of internment has been a massive escalation of violence (see Table 1). The total number of deaths by the end of 1975 directly resulting from political disorder was 1,391. The dead included hundreds of civilian bystanders, men and women, old and young, as well as 246 British soldiers, 131 police security officers, and hundreds of Republicans and scores of Loyalists killed "on active service" with illegal military units. The numbers injured have been greater: the security forces sustained more than 5,000 recorded injuries from 1968 up to the end of 1975, and civilians more than 10,000 injuries. Since the Troubles commenced in 1969, more than one Ulsterman in every hundred has been killed or wounded by political violence. Given the size of extended family networks in the Province, this means that nearly one family in every six has had a father, a son,

---

[6] For the British government's view, see Lord Gardiner, chairman, *Report of a Committee to consider, in the context of civil liberties and human rights, measures to deal with terrorism in Northern Ireland* (London: Her Majesty's Stationery Office, Cmnd. 5847, 1975); for a critical academic assessment, see K. Boyle, T. Hadden, and P. Hillyard, *Law and State: The Case of Northern Ireland* (London: Martin Robertson, 1975), Chapter 6.

## Table 1
### DEATHS BY POLITICAL VIOLENCE IN NORTHERN IRELAND, 1969–1975

| | Northern Ireland | | Great Britain [a] (equivalent annual) | United States [b] (equivalent annual) |
|---|---|---|---|---|
| | Annual | Cumulative total | | |
| 1969 | 13 | 13 | 455 | 1,794 |
| 1970 | 25 | 38 | 875 | 3,450 |
| 1971 | 173 | 211 | 6,055 | 23,874 |
| 1972 | 467 | 678 | 16,345 | 64,446 |
| 1973 | 250 | 928 | 8,750 | 34,500 |
| 1974 | 216 | 1,144 | 7,560 | 29,808 |
| 1975 | 247 | 1,391 | 8,645 | 34,085 |
| Totals | | | 48,685 | 191,958 |

[a] Assuming deaths in proportion to British population, 35 times that of Northern Ireland.
[b] Assuming deaths in proportion to U.S. population, 138 times that of Northern Ireland.
**Source:** Northern Ireland data: RUC Press Office, Belfast; British and American figures projected by the author.

a nephew or an aunt killed or injured in the Troubles. Moreover, British army search procedures subsequent to internment have resulted in up to 75,000 household searches per year in a society of some 400,000 households. In the period from summer 1969 through February 1973 an estimated 8,000 to 15,000 families, about 10 percent of the population of the greater Belfast area, were forced to move from their homes by threats of arson or shooting, because they were not of the religion dominant in their immediate neighborhoods. A disproportionate number of those intimidated were Catholics. The damage to property has been equally substantial, arising principally from more than 4,500 explosions set off in the Province from 1969 to the end of 1975 and more than 22,000 reported shooting incidents. As of 31 December 1975, a total of £133,945,686 had been paid out against claims for damage to property and £18,738,224 for personal injury claims. In addition, more than £60 million of damage claims were outstanding at this date.[7]

---

[7] For estimates of families forced from their homes, see John Darby and Geoffrey Morris, *Intimidation in Housing* (Belfast: Northern Ireland Community Relations Commission Research Paper, 1974). Figures on violence and property damage come from the RUC Press Office, Belfast.

The intensity and unexpectedness of the violence can be illustrated by some of the more notorious bombings and killings. On 4 December 1971, a bomb exploded at McGurk's bar in North Belfast, killing 15 people. On 30 January 1972 ("Bloody Sunday") British soldiers killed 13 young Catholic men when firing broke out during a civil rights demonstration in Londonderry. On Saturday, 4 March 1972, a bomb exploded among shoppers eating snacks in a crowded Belfast restaurant, the Abercorn, killing 2 women and injuring about 130, some of whom lost limbs in the explosion. On the afternoon of 21 July 1972 ("Bloody Friday") twenty-two bombs planted by the Provisional IRA exploded in Belfast, killing 9 people and injuring some 130. Of the seventy-eight members of the Stormont House of Commons and Senate in 1972, two have been murdered and at least three more have been the target of assassins.[8] While the peak number of deaths in 1972 has not been matched since, the total number of deaths keeps increasing, and there is no sign that violence is yet at an end. For example, forty-seven people died from political violence in the first month of 1976.

The small size of Northern Ireland might lead outsiders to regard the Province's casualty figures, while grim, as nonetheless tolerable in an era marked by violence everywhere in the Western world. Such a reaction would be wrong. First, it would misjudge the recent past of the Northern Ireland people. Not a single murder was reported in Northern Ireland in 1963, and only one each in 1964 and 1965. Since 1971, more often than not a killing has occurred each day. Political violence affects not only the direct victims, but also the order and security of many other persons. Anyone who has had a friend or relative injured or killed in a public house explosion will think twice before going out with a friend for a drink. Anyone who reads of a neighbor shot dead by a sectarian assassination gang solely because of his religion will move warily through areas dominated by "the other side." The violence in Ulster is more than an antisocial act; it is a political act, intended to destroy public order. It demonstrates, temporarily at least, the inability of the government of the day to provide the first element of civil government.

Some idea of the scale of Ulster's violence is given in Table 1, which shows the number of deaths that would have occurred had equivalent civil disorder arisen in Great Britain or the United States. The number of dead in Ulster is, proportionate to population, twice the losses that Britain suffered in the Boer War, and about twice the number of deaths suffered by U.S. forces in the Korean and Vietnam

---

[8] Fatalities compiled by author from press accounts.

wars combined. An empirical appreciation of the British and Irish reactions to Ulster-style violence is provided whenever a bomb inspired by the Ulster Troubles explodes somewhere else in the British Isles. The single most deadly incident of the Troubles occurred in Dublin on Friday, 17 May 1974, when car bombs, apparently planted by Protestant Loyalists, exploded, killing 26 people. On Thursday, 21 November 1974, bombs apparently of IRA origin exploded in two Birmingham pubs, killing 21 people and injuring 170 Englishmen. More than 50 people have been killed in explosions in Britain, and a similar number in the Republic of Ireland. While these numbers are small by Ulster standards, the deaths have produced a disproportionately strong reaction from British and Irish politicians. Although both states claim sovereignty over the territory of Northern Ireland, their leaders are unequivocal in asserting that the violence arising in Ulster should be kept there and not spread to the place where sovereignty is said to rest.

**The Political Vacuum, 1972–1975**

The British government entered Northern Ireland with the stated intention of making the Stormont system of government work as Westminster wished it to work. This wish was not shared by a majority of Ulstermen. Irish Republicans did not want to improve British rule, but to end it. Ultra-loyalists did not want to give Catholics greater influence, but to maintain the monopoly of power that they claimed, as of right, on the basis of free elections and allegiance to British principles of democracy, especially majority rule. The failure of the reforms to appease Catholic demands led Britain to turn its military force against the IRA, antagonizing the Catholic community as a whole; the failure of internment to stop IRA violence led Britain to stop its support of Stormont. Seven months after the introduction of internment in defense of the Stormont regime, the British government used its prerogative powers to suspend the Parliament of Northern Ireland, an act that effectively sentenced Stormont to extinction.

The responsibility for governing Northern Ireland fell by default to the British government at Westminster on 24 March 1972, when the Unionist administration of Brian Faulkner refused to accept British proposals to transfer responsibility for maintaining law and order to Westminster. Stormont was suspended because the British were no longer prepared to fight and be killed in defense of the Stormont regime.

The power to govern did not pass to Westminster with Britain's assumption of responsibility for direct rule of the Province. Instead, it sank almost out of sight. The power to govern is manifested in the successful discharge of the most elemental task of government: the maintenance of public order. The violence was far greater in the first twelve months of direct rule than in the last twelve months of the old Stormont regime. The number of reported shooting incidents rose from 2,837 to 11,574, and deaths from political violence rose from 243 to 464. Moreover, violence became three-sided: gun battles between the British-led defense forces and the IRA, bombing attacks by the IRA upon predominately Protestant shopping and residential areas, and Protestant retaliatory attacks, by bomb and bullet, against Catholics in Ulster.

In a temporary move to fill the vacuum left by the suspension of the Northern Ireland government, Britain put responsibility for governing in the hands of a secretary of state for Northern Ireland, a Westminster M.P. sitting in the British cabinet. The first incumbent of this post was a Conservative, William Whitelaw. The British House of Commons assumed legislative power for Northern Ireland as well as for Great Britain. Because Northern Ireland sends only 12 M.P.s to Westminster, its representatives are inevitably outvoted by the 623 British M.P.s. British dismay at the continuing violence in Ulster and the increasing loss of British lives there made it easy for Whitelaw and his successors to secure bipartisan support for British policy in Ulster, whether the policy of the moment involved conciliation or its traditional alternative, coercion.

An initial motive for the introduction of direct rule was to bring an end to the fighting between the British army and the IRA. To this purpose, Whitelaw achieved a brief truce in June 1972 after secret negotiations with Provisional IRA leaders in London. A month later, following the brutal IRA bombings of Bloody Friday, the British army carried out Operation Motorman, a military-style occupation of Republican-dominated "no go" areas in Belfast and Londonderry. The army's method of seeking security by firm, even ruthless, use of its coercive powers against large numbers of people was sanctioned by exceptional legislation suspending individual rights nominally ensured to British subjects and Irishmen by the European Convention on Human Rights. Of the 2,158 Ulstermen interned or held in custody without charge or trial because they were suspected of terrorist acts or associations, 95 percent have been Catholic.

The British government has had neither the will nor the force to govern the Province from London. It wishes to return government to the people of Northern Ireland. How to do so without intensifying violence and disorder is the problem that has faced Britain since March 1972. In the months following the introduction of direct rule, Whitelaw sought the views of all political groups in Northern Ireland about the best form of future government for the Province: there was no more consensus among them than there had been in the days of Stormont. Following an interparty conference at a secure hotel site in Darlington, England, in September 1972, the British Parliament passed a Constitution Act in March 1973 which provided for the return of a form of self-government to the Province. Under the plan set forth in this act, certain legislative functions would be transferred to a Northern Ireland Assembly, and certain executive functions to a Northern Ireland Executive. A novel feature, intended to secure Catholic influence and allegiance, was "power sharing." The act stipulated—in an attempt to end the power of the all-Protestant Unionist party—that the secretary of state for Northern Ireland would not sanction the formation of an Executive that consisted solely of a party drawing its support from only one community. The act also recognized the importance of "an Irish dimension" in Ulster politics and recommended the creation of institutions formally linking the Dublin, Belfast, and Westminster governments. The British government's plan was guardedly welcomed by the leaders of the two largest parties, Brian Faulkner of the Unionists and Gerry Fitt of the Catholic-based Social Democratic and Labour party (SDLP). They were denounced by more traditional Unionists and by Republicans.

The 26 June 1973 elections for the new Northern Ireland Assembly produced an ambiguous outcome: no party won a majority of the seventy-eight seats. The Protestant vote was split by the fragmentation of the Unionist party and the emergence of a new Loyalist Coalition opposed to Britain's terms. The Loyalists took twenty-seven seats with 35.4 percent of the vote and the Faulkner Unionists twenty-three seats with 26.5 percent of the vote. (See Table 2.) By late November, Whitelaw announced that three parties, together commanding a majority of votes in the seventy-eight-seat Assembly, had agreed to form a power-sharing Executive. The parties were Brian Faulkner's Protestant-based Unionist faction, the Catholic-based SDLP, and the Alliance party, which drew some of its smaller share of the vote from each community. The power-sharing Executive involved concessions from each party. The British government did not end internment, a major Catholic grievance, and Unionists were forced to sit in the cabinet with Catholics who still hoped for a peacefully united thirty-two-county Ireland. In December 1973, at

29

## Table 2
## NORTHERN IRELAND ASSEMBLY ELECTION RESULT, 1973

| Parties | Votes Number | Votes Percent of total | Number of Candidates | Number of Seats Won |
|---|---|---|---|---|
| Anti-White Paper Unionists | 89,759 | 12.4 | 15 | 11 |
| DUP (Paisleyites) | 78,228 | 10.8 | 17 | 8 |
| Vanguard | 75,759 | 10.5 | 25 | 7 |
| Other Loyalists | 11,660 | 1.6 | 8 | 1 |
| Total Loyalist | 255,406 | 35.4 | 65 | 27 |
| Faulkner Unionists | 191,729 | 26.5 | 41 | 23 |
| Alliance | 66,541 | 9.2 | 35 | 8 |
| Northern Ireland Labour | 18,675 | 2.6 | 18 | 1 |
| SDLP | 159,773 | 22.1 | 28 | 19 |
| Republican Clubs | 13,064 | 1.8 | 10 | 0 |
| Independent/others | 17,053 | 2.4 | 13 | 0 |
| Total non-Loyalist | | | 145 | 51 |
| TOTAL | 722,241 | 100.0 | 210 | 78 |

**Note:** The size of the electorate was 1,022,820. The size of the total vote was 739,093 (72.3 percent of the electorate) including 16,852 (2.3 percent) spoiled ballots.

**Source:** Ian McAllister, *The 1975 Northern Ireland Convention Election* (Glasgow: University of Strathclyde Survey Research Center, Occasional Paper 14, 1975), p. 15.

Sunningdale, a college near London, the British prime minister, Edward Heath, convened an unprecedented meeting of representatives of the new Executive and of the Irish and British governments. The Irish government made a nominal concession to Protestant opinion by announcing that it accepted the right of the Ulster people to self-determination, and the British government reciprocated by announcing that it would not oppose the unification of Ireland with the consent of a majority of Ulstermen. The Sunningdale conference agreed to the prompt establishment of a Council of Ireland to undertake responsibility for matters of common interest and concern to Ulster and the Republic.

The power-sharing Executive was launched in January 1974. Four days later the Unionist party rejected the arrangement, and Brian Faulkner resigned as leader of the party—but retained his position as chief minister in the Executive. The unexpected occurrence of a United Kingdom election on 28 February gave an early test of electoral opinion. Loyalist candidates who opposed the power-sharing Executive and the Sunningdale agreement won 51 percent of the vote and eleven of the twelve Northern Ireland seats at Westminster. Faulkner Unionists in favor of power sharing won 13 percent of the vote and the Catholic SDLP 22 percent. A National Opinion Polls survey conducted a month later found that 78 percent of Catholics strongly approved of power sharing, but only 28 percent of Protestants strongly approved.[9]

Four months after it had been created, the power-sharing Executive fell, following a fourteen-day general strike organized by the Protestant Ulster Workers' Council (UWC) to protest Britain's attempt to govern Northern Ireland through an Executive that excluded representatives of the ultra-loyalists, who claimed to represent a majority of the Protestant community. The strike, supported by various Protestant paramilitary groups, was nonviolent but extremely serious: it paralyzed Ulster by gradually withdrawing electrical power. The "revolutionary" demand of the Ulster Workers' Council was an immediate general election in the Province. Just as civil rights protest groups and subsequently the IRA had shown that extraconstitutional politics could destroy the old Stormont government, so Protestant strikers showed that protest tactics could be used to destroy a new-style British-sponsored system.[10]

The collapse of the Executive once more left government in British hands by default. However, the collapse of British policy in the face of the Ulster Workers' Council strike left many Ulster Protestants contemptuous of Britain's claims to influence events in the Province. The failure of the British government to use the British army against the strikers led Catholics to distrust Britain's commitment to their interests. The collapse of plans for a Council of Ireland led Dublin to distrust Britain's capability. Last and not least, the total failure of the power-sharing Executive led many British politicians to doubt their own ability ever to ensure government in the Province—with or without a desirable degree of consensus. This second suspension of an Ulster government in two years produced a political vacuum that has yet to be filled.

---

[9] *Political Opinion in Northern Ireland* (London: NOP Market Research Ltd., on behalf of BBC-TV Northern Ireland, 1974), p. 16.

[10] For an informed and detached account, see Robert Fisk, *The Point of No Return: The Strike which Broke the British in Ulster* (London: Andre Deutsch, 1975).

# 3

# THE PARTIES TO THE CONFLICT

*A fundamental problem since the earliest years of Northern Ireland's existence has been the disagreement not just about how Northern Ireland should be governed, but as to whether it should continue to exist at all.*

British Government White Paper, 1973

## Characteristics of Political Organization in Ulster

The parties to political debate in Ulster are not the organizations familiar to American or British politicians. While some organize to advance their aims by winning votes at elections, others use violence and are organized to do everything from providing armed defense of communities to carrying out assassinations and bombings. A few groups do both. These are dual-purpose movements, with one wing concentrating on electoral politics and another on violent politics. There are also protest groups that move back and forth in the shadowy world between what is formally legal and formally illegal.

To understand the politics of Northern Ireland, one must understand something about each group separately and recognize the coalitions that can be formed in efforts to govern or disrupt the government of the Province. Politicians who differ about everything including the constitution may nonetheless agree that their differences should be settled in a parliamentary fashion. Similarly, paramilitary groups in the two communities may share one assumption: that the ideals for which they fight can be justified by the political theory of "Mr. Colt," an Ulster euphemism for settling differences with guns.

For its size, Northern Ireland can claim more political organizations than any other society in the Western world. One reason for this is that almost any organization can be political—a football or hurley team, a folk song club, or a children's group that describes itself as a Protestant flute band. Individuals can belong to several groups at once or move in and out of a variety of organizations with bewildering speed. For example, one prominent Protestant politician has served two three-month jail sentences for leading protest demonstrations and has been deported from Italy for leading a protest against Protestant talks with the Vatican. Subsequently, he has consistently won masses of votes in his election campaigns. A leading member of the Social Democratic and Labour party was in the IRA and the Irish Labour party and then was chairman of the Northern Ireland Labour party, prior to becoming a founding member of the SDLP. While the party labels change, many of the faces behind them are familiar.

The intimate size of Northern Ireland, especially in the villages and countryside outside Belfast, throws politicians into frequent contact with each other and with officials of other organizations. M.P.s from opposing parties share drinks at the same bar in Stormont or in the hospitality room of a television company after a program. In their constituencies politicians rub shoulders with members of paramilitary organizations and with clergymen of their own faith, as well as with ordinary constituents looking for community leaders to help them with their personal problems. And they notice what "the other side" is doing to maintain or subvert civil government and public order.

**The Use of Arms.** Paramilitary groups in Ulster have a much longer history among both Catholics and Protestants than do political parties.[1] They were first formed in the eighteenth century, after the religious wars between English and continental European troops in seventeenth-century Ireland and before the introduction of a permanent nationwide police force in 1836. At their least organized, the groups of that day resembled the vigilantes or posses on the American frontier, ad hoc collections of friends and neighbors organized in self-defense to secure what they regarded as theirs by whatever rough and ready means were at hand, in the absence of settled and effective institutions of law and order. These groups, some public, others secret, persisted in the nineteenth century; they were involved in actions as carefully calculated as assassinations and rebellions and as

---

[1] See T. Desmond Williams, ed., *Secret Societies in Ireland* (Dublin: Gill & Macmillan, 1973) and Galen Broeker, *Rural Disorder and Police Reform in Ireland, 1812-36* (London: Routledge, 1970).

spontaneous as street riots. They came forward as the principal security forces in the guerrilla war fought in Ulster to keep the Province in the United Kingdom at the end of the First World War. Lord Brookeborough, prime minister of Ulster from 1943 until 1963, made his name politically as an organizer of an unofficial vigilante group in his native Fermanagh in 1920 and as a county commandant of the Ulster Special Constabulary. Similarly, presidents of the Irish Republic have been prominent ex-Republicans, like Eamon de Valera, or members of families whose political names were made in armed rebellion.

In Northern Ireland, paramilitary organizations lack the resources and training of full-time official armies. Most who serve in them do so only part time. They usually have equipment no heavier than what can be stored in their homes, in barns, or in small supply dumps dotted about the Province. Their chief weapons are guns and explosive mixtures required for bombs and, given modern technology, even these simple weapons can be lethal. Some of their weapons are stolen from government stores, others are imported, and others homemade. Paramilitary organizations, like political parties, can be vehicles for individual advancement as well as defenders of a cause. They finance their activities by robbing banks, operating illegal drinking clubs, and collecting "protection" money from taxicab drivers, shopkeepers, and anyone else who is vulnerable to intimidation. (Of 1,300 political prisoners imprisoned in mid-1975, 300 had been convicted on robbery charges.) The rewards of membership can be material as well as patriotic. But the risks are great. In addition to imprisonment or death at the hands of the regime's security forces, paramilitants also run the risk of being shot in the kneecap by their own officials for minor infractions of discipline, or being shot dead in internecine disputes.

**Sectarian Allegiances.** The best way to understand the nature of political organization in Northern Ireland is to think in terms of two categories of organizations, one within the Protestant community and the other within the Catholic community. Almost anyone starting a political group assumes that support will come from coreligionists, and any Protestant or Catholic wishing to become politically active will tend to look for an organization consisting of his own kind. This is almost as true of political parties as it is of paramilitary organizations. The effective choice facing most Ulstermen who are moved to take an interest in public affairs is whether to join a Protestant or a Catholic political party or paramilitary organization.

The importance of political allegiances formed along sectarian lines can readily be illustrated by an analysis of M.P.s elected to the Stormont House of Commons from its foundation in 1921 through 1969. In the twelve elections during that period, candidates appealing to Protestant voters under a variety of Unionist labels or to Catholics under a variety of Nationalist, Irish, or Republican labels won an average of forty-six of the forty-eight territorial seats.[2] Splits in the Unionist or Nationalist movement sometimes allowed an Ulsterman a choice between candidates of his own religion—but only in constituencies where a split would not risk letting the other side in. More often, an Ulsterman had no chance to vote at all, for an average of 37 percent of the seats were uncontested: in 1933 a high of 63 percent was reached.

Economic issues, the stuff of party politics elsewhere in Britain, have been subsidiary themes in Ulster politics. The Unionist party, while officially allied with the Conservative party in England, has never made free enterprise a campaign issue. To do so would be to risk stimulating manual workers to vote Labour. Instead, it has campaigned on the constitution, an issue that unites Protestants across class lines. Moreover, the Northern Ireland government's practice of step-by-step adoption of social legislation introduced at Westminster has meant that the Unionists received credit for introducing at Stormont welfare-state legislation brought in by the 1945–51 Labour government in Britain. Moreover, Ulster welfare benefits— disproportionately high because of a high incidence of unemployment and of large families drawing family allowances from the state— have been subsidized by the British taxpayer. The Northern Ireland Labour party has always sought and never succeeded in attracting votes on straight "left-right" economic grounds. It never won more than three seats until it came off the fence on the issue of the constitution and endorsed the link with Britain in 1949. Its strength reached a maximum of four seats at the 1958 and 1962 elections. The Catholic community has been more fissiparous because of weak party organization. In Catholic areas of Belfast, candidates have sometimes won seats fighting under a Labour or Socialist label—but with the term Republican or Irish annexed.

Organizations that seek to unite Protestants and Catholics have always been weak in their electoral support. For example, trade unions may withdraw from electoral activity in order to avoid losing members whose common interests on one issue, such as employment,

---

[2] Until 1969 the remaining four M.P.s in Stormont were elected by a constituency consisting of graduates of Queen's University, Belfast.

are not matched by agreement about constitutional matters. Those organizations that seek support in terms of two causes—unionism or Irish nationalism plus economic or other interests—find their support diminished because they appeal to only a fraction of one community. By comparison, if they confine their appeal to constitutional issues, they increase their potential support by including middle-class and working-class coreligionists.

## Protestant Political Groupings

The politics of the Protestant community has been dominant in Northern Ireland since 1921 for a simple reason: Protestants constitute two-thirds of the electorate. As long as constitutional issues remain central to electoral politics, rotation of parties in office, following more or less pendulum-like swings in popular opinion, does not occur.

**The Unionists.** The Ulster Unionist party was the electoral organization translating the Protestant majority in the population into a Protestant majority in the Stormont Parliament.[3] By representing a majority of Ulster voters, the Unionist party won control of the Stormont government. By controlling government, Protestants could determine policies governing the whole population. The Orange Order provided a third institutional base for Protestant political activity, organizing Ulstermen to defend their religion by whatever means necessary. As long as the party of Orangemen governed in accord with Orange principles, the order had no need to pursue an independent political line.

The iron triangle of Unionist party-Stormont government-Orange Order was breached during the leadership of Terence O'Neill in the late 1960s and fell apart under pressure from civil rights campaigners, the British government, and IRA violence. First of all, the Unionist party was divided about O'Neill's policy of conciliating Catholics. When his initiatives were followed by civil rights demonstrations rather than by a show of Catholic allegiance, O'Neill lost his grip on the party and fell from office in 1969. In 1972–73, the Unionists divided about the desirability of sharing power, first of all with the British government and then, under British supervision, with Catholic politicians in Ulster. Concurrently, Unionists divided about the appropriateness of maintaining membership in an exclusively

---

[3] For a detailed history, with useful appendices, see John Harbinson, *The Ulster Unionist Party, 1882-1973* (Belfast: Blackstaff, 1973).

Protestant Orange Order while appealing for votes in an electorate that is one-third Catholic. Only after the expulsion of Brian Faulkner, the party's leader and head of the power-sharing Executive in 1974, did the Unionist party regain a modicum of unity. But by this time, other electoral parties had formed among Protestants, claiming to represent a truer, harder, more "loyal" point of view.

In 1975, three political parties grouped under the heading of the United Ulster Unionist Council (UUUC) or Loyalist Coalition jointly claimed themselves heirs to the traditions of Ulster Unionism—and to the powers that the Unionist party had long enjoyed at Stormont. The fact that the official Unionists, the Democratic Unionist party (DUP), and the Vanguard Unionist party (VUP) are separately organized testifies to the fissiparous tendencies of personalities and events as well as principles. Their coalition unity is testimony to the value that Protestants place upon determining their political future by winning an electoral majority. The common description of the coalition as Loyalist rather than Unionist emphasizes the priority given to loyalty to Ulster rather than to union with a British government whose intentions toward Ireland are uncertain.

The contemporary Ulster Unionist party, the historic party of Ulster Protestants, was founded in 1892 to organize Ulster Protestant opposition to the British government's acceptance of Irish home rule. From 1921 until the suspension of Stormont its leader was also the prime minister of Northern Ireland. Article III of the party constitution states its aim: "to maintain Northern Ireland as an integral part of the United Kingdom: to uphold and defend the Constitution and Parliament of Northern Ireland." The Unionists are a single-claim party, advancing no distinctive principles or programs other than maintaining the union with Britain. None of the party's leaders would call himself a socialist—though all would welcome government assistance in the form of British treasury subsidies for everything from Ulster shipyards to Ulster pig farms. The issues crucial to the party's unity are not defined in economic terms. For example, Enoch Powell, a leading British exponent of right-wing economic views, became a Unionist M.P. at Westminster in 1974 because he had forthrightly insisted upon the "Britishness" of Ulster; he is regularly attacked by Unionist colleagues whenever he rashly suggests that the principles of free enterprise recommend an end to British government subsidies to Northern Ireland.

The Unionist party has a well-established party organization throughout Ulster, but it also bears scars arising from the splits within the party that led to the overthrow of three successive leaders,

Terence O'Neill, James Chichester-Clark, and Brian Faulkner. Each of these leaders was deposed because he was prepared to accept British terms for retaining Northern Ireland within the United Kingdom rather than to uphold and defend the terms of union preferred by the majority in the party's councils. The party's present leader, Harry West, a farmer from Fermanagh, represents the traditional Loyalist outlook: "While we proclaim loyalty to the British Crown, we do not necessarily follow the dictates of any British political party at Westminster."[4]

**The DUP.** The Democratic Unionist party is the political wing of the movement led by the Rev. Dr. Ian R. K. Paisley,[5] head of the Free Presbyterian Church, which he has built up in two decades of evangelism in Ulster. In the mid-1960s, Paisley organized a protest group, the Ulster Constitution Defense Committee. It was ultra-loyal, pledged "to maintain the Constitution at all costs. When the authorities [that is, the government of the day] act contrary to the Constitution the body will take whatever steps it thinks fit to expose such unconstitutional acts."[6] Paisley personally led protest demonstrations against Republican activities, civil rights marches, and alleged "romanizing" tendencies in the Presbyterian Church. In February 1969 he entered electoral politics, and his organization nominated five candidates for the Stormont election as Protestant Unionists. In 1970 he was elected to the Westminster House of Commons and, at a by-election, won the Stormont seat vacated by the resignation of Terence O'Neill. In 1971 his political followers regrouped under the name of the Democratic Unionist party and won eight seats in the 1973 Assembly election.

While Paisley is not the only clergyman active in Ulster politics, he is the best known. A man who has built up a large following through evangelical preaching, he and his party attract support from traditionally apolitical Protestants who are worried not only about the threat of a possible Irish takeover of Ulster, but also about a possible Roman Catholic takeover of Protestant churches through the worldwide ecumenical movement. Constitutionally, the DUP has been distinctive in advocating the advantages of closer integration with Westminster, including an increase in Northern Ireland's representation in the British Parliament to give it parity with Scotland and

---

4 See "Powell Talking Nonsense—Paisley," *Belfast Telegraph,* 7 July 1975.
5 Paisley's doctorate is an honorary degree awarded by the fundamentalist Bob Jones University, Greenville, South Carolina.
6 Quoted in The Cameron Commission, *Disturbances in Northern Ireland,* p. 119.

Wales. The prefix *Democratic* in the party's title signifies a populist bias in party pronouncements. For example, Paisley shows concern about poor housing conditions and employment problems in the Province as well as about constitutional matters. Inevitably, the party's policies are defined by the statements made by Paisley, whose bulky figure looms large in Ulster politics as well as within his party. Paisley is sufficiently confident of his judgment to follow an independent line when he deems this appropriate—for example, in criticizing internment, whether applied to Catholics, Protestants, or both. He gives a traditional Ulster definition of loyalty:

> We hold no allegiance whatsoever to the Wilsons and Heaths of this world. Our fathers rejected the attempts of the British Parliament, swayed by Irish Nationalists, to force home rule on Ireland.
>
> If the Crown in Parliament decreed to put Ulster into a United Ireland, we would be disloyal to Her Majesty if we did not resist such a surrender to our enemies.[7]

**Vanguard.** The Vanguard Unionist party (VUP) was founded under the leadership of William Craig in March 1973 as a breakaway from Brian Faulkner's Unionist party. Craig had been a Unionist M.P. at Stormont since 1960 and a cabinet minister until he fell out with Terence O'Neill about accepting British government advice on security matters in 1968. The creation of the Vanguard Unionist party followed the creation in February 1972 of Ulster Vanguard as a loyalist pressure group whose tactics included massive street marches and token work stoppages to protest the suspension of the Stormont Parliament. Craig used his established position within the Unionist party to stump the Province, seeking support for his views before setting up the Vanguard Unionists. The party thus started with a network of contacts throughout Northern Ireland. In the June 1973 Assembly election, it won seven seats.

The Vanguard Unionists are distinctive in two ways. First, the party has stated that an independent Ulster might be the most realistic means of maintaining the Province's British heritage. William Craig has expressed the Vanguard outlook thus:

> We would prefer to maintain the Union but the desire must be reciprocated, and pledges must be accompanied by a powerful Parliament in Northern Ireland to resist all attacks and to defeat the inevitable recurring terrorist on-

---

[7] "Loyalist Attack on Powell," *Irish Times*, 7 July 1975.

slaughts virtually guaranteed to take place by the success of the present [1973 IRA] attack.

If there is not to be this strength in the United Kingdom we would prefer to be outside the United Kingdom, seeking no special treatment but expecting at least the same consideration as the anti-British South when it opted out.[8]

The party's symbol—the red hand of Ulster—is chosen to emphasize that its commitment to Ulster nationalism is greater than that of the Official Unionists or the Democratic Unionists. Second, Vanguard is distinctive in maintaining open contact with Protestant paramilitary groups. Ulster Vanguard sits on the Ulster Loyalist Central Coordinating Committee, along with representatives of the Ulster Defence Association, the Province's largest paramilitary group, and trade union shop stewards ready to call factory strikes for political ends. Craig has termed it "regrettable, but justifiable and necessary that we should be concerned with what could be termed war plans. If there is a change imposed on Ulster we shall fight and defeat it." He argues that the electoral tactics of Vanguard offer an alternative to "an appalling bloodbath." [9]

**The Orange Order.** Founded in 1795, the Orange Order is the oldest continuously active political organization in Northern Ireland, although it is not organized like a political party, nor does it contest elections.[10] It is important because it unites in one institution Protestants who are otherwise divided among a number of denominations, as well as the one-third of the Protestant community who rarely or never go to church. Approximately one-third of Protestant men belong to the Orange Order, which has lodges throughout the Province. It thus provides both a local meeting place and a means for like-minded people to combine to influence parties and government in Belfast. The order sees itself as a religious and charitable association, favoring strict Sabbatarianism, conservative interpretations of the Bible, regularity in church attendance, and fellowship and mutual help among Orangemen. An Orangeman's oath pledges him, among other things, to "avoid countenancing by his presence or otherwise any act or ceremony of Popish worship." It is thus opposed strongly to any

---

[8] William Craig, *The Future of Northern Ireland* (Belfast: United Loyalist Council pamphlet, 1973), p. 9.

[9] William Craig, *First Anniversary Rally Speech* (Belfast: Ulster Vanguard pamphlet, 1973), p. 6.

[10] For an unemotional and informed account of the Orange Order's role in the Unionist party, see Harbinson, *Ulster Unionist Party*, Chapter 8.

links between Northern Ireland and the Catholic-oriented Republic of Ireland, and its political pronouncements express Loyalist views.

In an exclusively Protestant country, the Orange Order would be an old-fashioned patriotic organization, recalling the heroic deeds and famous speeches of the country's founding fathers. In Northern Ireland, it is patriotic in the eyes of one community, but a symbol of intimidation to the other. The order annually organizes marches to commemorate King William of Orange's victory at the Battle of the Boyne on 12 July 1690. "The Twelfth" is the Ulster Protestant's equivalent to the American Fourth of July or the Catholic commemoration of the 1916 Easter Monday rising against the British in Dublin. These marches remind both communities which side won the war that has determined the governance of Ulster ever since. The Orange Order nominates 122 members to the Unionist party's ruling council. It also has many members in Unionist constituency associations. Until the O'Neill era, nearly every Unionist M.P. was also a member of the Orange Order. This demonstrates that Orangemen disagree about many things, for disputes were frequent among Unionists in the old Stormont Parliament. Exceptionally, the grand master of the Orange Order, the Rev. Martin Smyth, sits as an Official Unionist in the Convention.

The Orange Order is a pressure group, not a political party. Orangemen are found in a variety of Ulster political parties and paramilitary groups. Because so large a proportion of the Protestant community belongs to the Orange Order, its members represent a range of views; they do not agree among themselves on all matters. The unity of the order has been maintained through the years by concentrating upon those few principles that unite Orangemen, rather than upon the many issues about which they differ. The tendency of the Orange Order is to emphasize traditional Loyalist views. In the words of its Belfast grand master: "Thank God our loyalty is not to any particular Westminster government but to the throne, which is above squalid party politics." [11]

**The UPNI.** The Unionist party of Northern Ireland (UPNI) was formed in early May 1974 by Brian Faulkner, who for twenty-five years previously had sat as an Official Unionist at Stormont and had held cabinet posts since 1959. Like Vanguard, the UPNI was a breakaway from the Official Unionist party organization—but a break in the opposite direction. Faulkner had himself come to power at

[11] "Ulster Storm on Powell Definition of 'Loyalty,'" The *Times* (London), 7 July 1975.

Stormont by exploiting Unionist divisions from the Loyalist side. As prime minister and subsequently as leader of the short-lived 1974 power-sharing Executive, he was subject to British government pressure to depart from traditional Loyalist policies. In the June 1973 Assembly election, the Unionist party was badly divided by Faulkner's willingness to go along with a British White Paper endorsing power sharing with Catholics. From a position within the official organization, Faulkner was able to secure the election of twenty-three candidates pledged to his point of view. But the price he paid was the election of eleven anti-Faulkner Unionists and sixteen Loyalists. (See Table 2.) Faulkner was thus in a minority within the traditional Unionist and Loyalist community. His overthrow as Official Unionist leader followed in January 1974.

The Unionist party of Northern Ireland was founded as an Assembly-based party, rather than a constituency-based party. Its first members were ex-Unionists who had sat in the Assembly and in Stormont for years previously. Many also held ministerial posts in the power-sharing Executive. The UPNI goes further than the other three parties that incorporate the word Unionist in their titles: it not only emphasizes the importance of maintaining Northern Ireland as part of the United Kingdom, but also expresses readiness to develop institutions of governance consistent with the wishes of the Westminster Parliament. It has disagreed with the Loyalist view that Ulstermen alone have the right to determine how the Province should be governed and to oppose or reject institutions laid down by a British Parliament. Article 2 of the UPNI Constitution endorses "the principle of agreed coalition" and "democratic participation by all sections of the community." These principles were used to justify UPNI politicians' sharing power with Catholics in 1974—but they leave open both the means by which power sharing might occur in the future and the question of whether the views of Catholic-based parties about power sharing would match the UPNI interpretation of such principles.

**Government Security Forces.** Until the British army entered Northern Ireland in 1969, Ulster Protestants had no need to organize paramilitary groups to compete with or complement the work of political parties. The Stormont government was responsible for security within the Province, and Protestants identified it as "their" government. The Royal Ulster Constabulary, the principal security organization in the Province, was the responsibility of such Unionist ministers of home affairs as Brian Faulkner and William Craig. The force was 90 percent

Protestant and indubitably "loyal." A branch of the Ulster Special Constabulary, the B Specials, was composed of Ulstermen who were recruited into government service on a part-time basis and were prepared to guard installations that were likely IRA targets, to set up road blocks, and to patrol areas where rebel activity was expected. B Specials were uniformed and armed reservists, in some ways analogous to American National Guardsmen called upon to handle race riots or massive protest demonstrations. Like National Guardsmen, they were part-time security officers, lacking the training and discipline of full-time soldiers. The B Specials were 100 percent Protestant. Politically active Catholics often complained of bias and discrimination in the policing policies of the Stormont security forces. These forces maintained public order with little loss of life, by comparison with the loss of life that has occurred since 1969.

The civil rights demonstrations of 1968 presented novel problems to Stormont's security forces, which failed to respond successfully at every level from the minister of home affairs downwards. The actions of the RUC and of the B Specials in attacking demonstrators or not intervening when Protestant crowds attacked demonstrators led to considerable criticism of the Stormont government in Britain and finally, in the Bogside rising of 12 August 1969, to a breakdown of public order that internal security forces could not contain. The British army entered the Province to end the violence. In October 1969, a British-directed report on policing recommended the disbandment of the B Specials and a change of the RUC's role from that of an armed unit, fulfilling military or quasi-military functions, to that of an unarmed force concerned with "normal" police problems.[12] The security of the Stormont regime henceforth rested in the hands of the British government and overall responsibility for the maintenance of public order in the Province with the British army.

Public order has not followed (see Table 1). Protestants concerned with their security—both as individuals subjected to the effects of IRA violence and as a community fearful of being bombed into an Irish Republic—have been unable to act as they wished within the framework of the lawfully established security forces. Until the suspension of Stormont, the Unionist government could lobby British security forces to intensify their efforts against the IRA. Since March 1972, the British government has reserved to itself security

---

[12] For a historical perspective, see Sir Arthur Hezlet, *The 'B' Specials* (London: Tom Stacey, 1972). For a prescription of what policing ought to be like, see *Report of the Advisory (Hunt) Committee on Police in Northern Ireland* (Belfast: Her Majesty's Stationery Office, Cmnd. 535, 1969).

decisions affecting Ulstermen. Protestants concerned about the failure of the British government's policies have turned to paramilitary organizations controlled by their own men.

**Protestant Paramilitary Groups.** In Northern Ireland, paramilitary organizations compete with government for what is usually considered a government monopoly: the use of force to maintain order. The crucial political feature of the paramilitary organizations is not their reliance upon military weapons, which is equally characteristic of the British army and the RUC. It is their readiness to undertake security operations and use weapons without the authority of the regime behind them. They see these actions as a supreme expression of political commitment: they are prepared to kill and die to promote what they believe or to prevent what they oppose. They challenge the British government to decide whether the ideals to which they are loyal and the activities in which they engage are lawful or not. In the light of Ulster politics, they might best be said to occupy a shadowy world between the legal and the illegal. Only a few of the smaller groups have been specifically proscribed by law.

Because paramilitary organizations sometimes engage in extralegal or illegal activities, such as military drill, bomb attacks, assassinations, and fund-raising activities outside the law, their organization and operations are only imperfectly known. Moreover, an individual can participate in more than one organization, and nomenclature can vary more or less randomly from one part of the Province to another. Collectively, armed Protestants do not constitute anything as organized or coordinated as an army; rather, they are a collection of armed bands and their supporters; forty-six differently denominated groups have been identified to date. This situation can best be understood in terms of the functions that can be undertaken by a host of organizations more or less specifically identified by the names of paramilitary groups.

*Community defense.* The increasing violence of IRA attacks in 1971–72 led anxious Protestants to lose confidence in British assurances that established security forces of the regime were adequate to defend their homes and communities. Throughout Ulster a variety of local defense associations sprang up, the counterparts of defense organizations created in Catholic communities following the violence of August 1969. In urban areas, defense groups have a clearly defined task: to patrol neighborhood streets at night, using barricades to establish checkpoints for motorists. Because each force is local, it has no difficulty in distinguishing friends and neighbors from strangers. In the countryside, patrols operate on rural roads and guard buildings that are subject to arson or bomb attack, such as Orange halls. Community defense associations need not carry arms, insofar as patrols and barricades are meant to serve as "tripwires" or "deterrents." A group of Ulstermen with cudgels, shillelaghs, and other homemade implements can be intimidating even without firearms. The more precarious the security of a community, the more necessary is an arsenal of some sort.

Outside a neighborhood, defense organizations become significant insofar as they are affiliated with Ulster-wide bodies, such as the Ulster Special Constabulary Association, an organization of individuals who formerly served in the B Specials, or the Ulster Defence Association (UDA), which is linked with the Vanguard movement. These organizations can, upon occasion, call out 10,000 men or more to take part in mass rallies or even more striking paramilitary parades. The show of men marching in military formation is meant to remind enemies that volunteers stand ready to defend their ideal of Ulster, should the British army no longer be prepared to do so.

*Attack.* Within a community of men organized to repel IRA attacks, there are always a few who believe that a waiting game is inadequate, that the best way to defend the community is to eliminate the perceived cause of the danger, Republican gunmen. Since 1972 small Protestant groups have been acting upon this belief, assassinating or attempting to assassinate Catholics suspected of IRA activities, placing bombs with lethal consequences in public houses frequented by Catholics, shooting Catholics associating "improperly" with Protestants (married to Protestants, for example, or working in jobs that Protestants feel should go to coreligionists), or simply attacking Catholics more or less at random because "they are all Fenians [that is, rebels] anyway." The least discriminate Protestant attacks, like their IRA equivalents, have overtones of pure racial conflict, as expressed in lines from "I Was Born under the Union Jack," a song of the Shankill Defence Association, an extreme Loyalist group: "You've never seen a better Taig [slang for Catholic] than with a bullet in his back." The publisher of these lyrics was prosecuted under the Incitement to Hatred Act. The prosecution was not successful.

In the world of Ulster politics, killings are only officially recorded as sectarian assassinations when a spokesman for a group telephones a newspaper or the police to claim a murder as its own work. The number and character of the groups at the far end of the telephone are cloudy—but more than 200 Catholics have undoubtedly died at their hands. (About 150 Protestants have been killed in assassinations undertaken by Republican groups.) The Ulster Volunteer Force was first to strike; its leader killed a Catholic barman suspected of IRA sympathies in 1966. Masked men claiming to be UVF spokesmen have also claimed responsibility for killing Catholics (and Protestants) during the Troubles of the 1970s. Elite groups with names such as the Ulster Freedom Fighters and the Protestant Action Force have been organized within broader-based paramilitary organizations.[13]

*Fighting for a "new Ulster."* While it is misleading to describe people fighting for a Protestant and British Ulster as nonpolitical, most nonetheless see themselves in this light—that is, they do not take sides on the social and economic issues that conventionally divide parties in Britain and America. In this way paramilitary groups avoid becoming entangled with electoral parties; they are nonpartisan, though hardly apolitical. They can seek recruits regardless of their attitudes toward housing, education, welfare payments, or a host of other issues. To introduce class politics is to confine a group's potential support base to manual workers or to the middle class, as well as to alienate those for whom conventional constitutional issues are the only spur to political action. Moreover, class appeals would imply that Protestant workers might have a common cause with Catholic workers—a proposition that Ulstermen have always found difficult to believe, though there has never been a shortage of native and imported idealists seeking to convince them that it is true.

A few paramilitary groups have pronounced themselves dissatisfied with social and economic conditions and have added social and economic goals to their traditional constitutional concerns. For example, the Volunteer Political party, an offshoot of the Ulster Volunteer Force, was formed in April 1974 shortly after the UVF was removed from the list of organizations declared illegal by the British government. Its manifesto for the October 1974 Westminster election declared, "In the past our representatives have paid very little attention to Ulster's economy. Those days are now over." Its leader, Kenneth Gibson, a candidate in West Belfast, took but 6 percent of the total vote, only one in every seven Protestant votes. The Volunteer Political party has been heard of no more, and the UVF has again emphasized an active military policy, leading once more to its proscription as an illegal organization in October 1975.

---

[13] See Martin Dillon and Denis Lehane, *Political Murder in Northern Ireland* (Harmondsworth: Penguin Special, 1973). More generally, see Sarah Nelson, "Protestant 'Ideology' Considered," in Ivor Crewe, ed., *British Political Sociology Yearbook*, vol. 2 (London: Croom Helm, 1975).

*Industrial action for political ends.* In the mythology of class politics, a general strike is often invoked as a means to bring about a revolution. Northern Ireland is the only country in Western Europe where a successful general strike for political ends has occurred in the past generation, but that strike was not in the name of the working class, but rather in the name of the Loyalists. Political protest strikes began in March 1972, under the sponsorship of LAW (Loyalist Association of Workers), a part of the Vanguard movement. The strikes were initially in protest against the failure of British security forces to stop the IRA's bombing campaign. Because LAW included workers in electricity generating stations, the effects of the strikes were widespread, albeit confined to a period of a few hours.

The most dramatic and successful strike was organized by the Ulster Workers' Council in May 1974—a general strike threatening electricity, gas, sewage, and other essential services. The council consisted of individuals prominent in trade unions within the Province, including such major British unions as the Engineers and the Transport and General Workers. Union headquarters do not formally endorse such strikes—but their members do and are not penalized for doing so by their unions. The Ulster Workers' Council operated in collaboration with a variety of paramilitary groups. The level of armed violence dropped during the strike as Protestant groups concentrated their efforts upon an intimidating display of industrial action. The British army did not seek to test the strength of the armed force behind the strikers by attempting to break a strike that the British prime minister had denounced as intolerable. The strikers achieved their immediate aim: the downfall of the power-sharing Executive. The Executive collapsed when Brian Faulkner resigned after the British government refused to open talks with the UWC on the fourteenth day of the strike.[14]

Loyalist political groups—whether electoral parties or paramilitary organizations—dominate the politics of the Protestant community. Election results as well as tabulations of the incidence of violence make this evident. Most groups share a number of aims: a desire for majority rule within Northern Ireland and for maintenance of ties with Britain. They also share common enemies: the IRA and the Republic of Ireland.

Analytically, the various Protestant political organizations appear complementary. There are three Loyalist electoral parties, each with a slightly different nuance to its Loyalism, plus a variety of defensive

---

[14] See Fisk, *The Point of No Return,* for an account of the organization of the strikers and inaction by the British government and army.

and offensive paramilitary organizations and a group of industrial workers whose ability to paralyze the working life of the Province has been demonstrated. In practice, however, individual organizations rarely work together for long with other groups. Differences in structure, in appeal, and in leading personalities make cooperation difficult, except when the benefits are immediate and great. Protestant paramilitary groups have established coordinating committees that include representatives drawn from up to six different organizations. Nonetheless, organizations such as the UVF and free-lance gunmen continue to pursue their own policies when and as they choose. The Loyalist Coalition (UUUC) formed during the Convention electoral campaign has demonstrated the ability to agree upon slates of candidates to maximize electoral effectiveness. But the existence of three separate parties within the coalition is evidence of differences that are important between elections; this was clearly demonstrated in the first six months of the Convention. (See Chapter 6.) The Vanguard movement, founded to coordinate electoral campaigns, paramilitary work, and industrial action, has failed to achieve its aim consistently. At different times, each side of the movement seizes the initiative, leaving the other side to follow—much as different wings of the British Labour movement or the American Democratic party act independently of each other. During the 1974 general strike organized by the UWC, elected politicians were rarely to be seen—or welcomed— at the headquarters of the strikers. Reciprocally, in preparations for the Convention election of 1975, paramilitary organizations were rebuffed in their efforts to increase their influence within the UUUC. Each organization has its distinctive capabilities—whether it is winning votes or killing Taigs. The failure of the UVF's electoral candidate is a reminder of what can happen when a paramilitary group "goes political," weighing its influence with ballots. The intimidating sight of thousands of men marching in military formation down the main avenue of Belfast, however, is a reminder that bullets, not ballots, may be the final arbiter of the fate of the Protestant community.

## Catholic Political Groupings

Politically, Catholics have faced a common problem: how to act when numbers confine them to a minority status within a Northern Ireland state whose boundaries were intentionally drawn to make their minority status permanent. There has been little agreement among Catholics about an appropriate response. In a survey taken in 1968 shortly before the Troubles began, 33 percent of Catholics said that they supported the Stormont constitution, primarily because of its material benefits and efficiency, 34 percent rejected it because they preferred a united Ireland or considered the constitution unfair to Catholics, and 32 percent were "don't knows." While the proportions accepting, rejecting, or uncertain about the constitution change through time, each of these groups remain significant within the Catholic community. There are also persisting and changing differences of opinion about compliance with basic political laws. In 1968, 40 percent of Catholics approved of illegal protest demonstrations by Republicans and 13 percent approved of using "any measures," including violence, to achieve a united Ireland. While Protestants have been almost unanimous in their desire to maintain the border between Northern Ireland and the Republic, Catholics have been divided: there has been no Catholic majority either for accepting the border as final or for intensifying efforts to abolish it.[15]

In the era of Stormont, the politics of the Catholic community of Northern Ireland was based on the assumption of exclusion from office. Exclusion has usually resulted from numerical weakness: Catholics constitute one-third of the electorate in a British-style parliamentary system in which majorities rule. Sometimes, however, the Catholics' exclusion has been self-imposed. Republican candidates have won election on an abstention platform, promising not to attend a British Parliament on the grounds that Ulstermen should only be governed from Dublin. The chief political institutions of the era of exclusion were the Nationalist party, the Republican movement, and the Catholic Church. For decades, these gave structure to the self-contained politics of the Catholic community of Northern Ireland.

**The Nationalists.** The Nationalist party reflected the traditional aspiration for the unity of the thirty-two counties of Ireland, and little else. Its lack of a social program for an economically depressed Province led critics to describe the Nationalists as Green Tories. In circumstances in which two-thirds of the population opposed an end to the border, its policy was self-defeating in electoral terms. The Nationalists recognized this, nominating only a dozen or so candidates for the fifty-two constituencies of the Stormont Parliament, usually contesting only seats that a Catholic was sure to win. The Nationalists had a traditionally appealing label, but no organization. The party never had a headquarters and did not hold an annual party conference until 1966. At Stormont the Nationalists had little influence: their one legislative triumph was the passage of an act concerning

---

[15] For survey details, see Rose, *Governing without Consensus*, Chapters 5-6.

wild birds in 1931. Although the second largest party in the Stormont Parliament, the Nationalists refused to take the title of Loyal Opposition because it was to Cathleen ni Houlihan (a poetic symbol of Ireland) rather than to Queen Elizabeth II that they were loyal.

**Republican Organizations.** The Republican movement, with headquarters in Dublin, has provided multiple alternatives to Stormont politics. The IRA had a minute membership in Northern Ireland from the mid-1920s until the revival of the Troubles in 1969. So indifferent were Ulster Catholics to IRA campaigns that the Republicans gave lack of popular support among Catholics as a major reason for ending their campaign of 1956–1962.[16] Sinn Fein, its electoral wing, was barred from participating in Stormont elections in 1934 because its members refused to take an oath to attend sessions of the Stormont Parliament. It could, however, through an electoral anomaly, contest elections for the Westminster Parliament. In 1955, Sinn Fein candidates won two of the twelve Ulster seats in the British Parliament but did not wish to attend its sittings—nor could they, as both were serving prison sentences for their Republican activities. The Gaelic Athletic Association (GAA), founded in the Republic of Ireland as part of the Nationalist movement, has historically been the largest Republican-oriented organization in Ulster; its popularity arises from its sports program, involving competitions on a thirty-two-county basis. Until 1970 the GAA forbade its members to play "English" games such as rugby football and cricket. The GAA offers symbolic allegiance to Republican ideals; for example, the chief GAA stadium in Northern Ireland, Roger Casement Park in Belfast, is named after an Anglo-Irishman executed by the British for his part in the Irish rebellion.

**The Catholic Church.** Under Stormont rule, as under previous regimes, the Catholic Church has been the one organization catering to nearly all members of the minority community. In Northern Ireland Catholic churchgoing is measured in terms of weekly attendance (62 percent) or more frequent attendance (33 percent). The parochial organization of the church covers the whole of the Province, and church schools and social facilities provide for parishioners of all

---

[16] For the definitive history of the IRA from the end of the Irish civil war to the time of the recent Ulster Troubles, see J. Bowyer Bell, *The Secret Army* (London: Blond, 1970). For developments since, see Sunday Times Insight Team, *Ulster* (Harmondsworth: Penguin, 1972), and for the views of an interested party, see Sean MacStiofain, *Memoirs of a Revolutionary* (London: Gordon Cremonesi, 1975).

ages. The Catholic hierarchy as such rarely expresses views about political matters, except such distinctively Catholic concerns as church control of schools. Because the clergy are drawn from Northern Ireland and live daily with the problems of the Province, they reflect, in the variety of their outlooks, the opinions found within their flocks. Individual priests and bishops can be heard to endorse almost every view found within the Catholic community. Their identification with the community has meant that the bulk of Catholic priests disapproved of the Stormont regime and have supported the ideal of a united Ireland.[17]

**The Civil Rights Movement.** The Catholic community broke out of its isolation with the launching of a civil rights campaign in 1968. The campaign was novel because it accepted, de facto at least, the status of Northern Ireland as part of the United Kingdom. It sought *British* rights for Ulster Catholics. The demands included such "welfare rights" as better housing and full employment, as well as specifically political rights (for example, "one man, one vote, one value" and an end to restrictions upon political organizations such as Republican Clubs). The constitution of the Northern Ireland Civil Rights Association gave most prominence to political rights. The civil rights campaign was also novel in that its leaders offered an alternative to two traditional forms of Ulster Catholic political activity, losing elections and losing IRA gunbattles with security forces. Civil rights groups organized massive street marches to demonstrate their opposition to the status quo in Ulster, and the marches were held whether the Stormont government granted permits or declared them illegal. The violence of Protestant counter-demonstrators and, upon occasion, of the RUC generated international publicity and considerable sympathy in Britain and America for the civil rights campaigners.

The civil rights campaign was also distinctive in its leadership. In place of veteran Nationalist or Republican politicians, many of its leaders were younger Catholics who were less concerned with traditions than with the present problems of Ulster. They sought action *now*—rather than at the distant date of a Republican millenium. In doing this, the civil rights campaigners did not eschew aspirations for a united Ireland, but they avoided reference to them when it would merely inflame Protestant opinion. Civil rights campaigners were

---

[17] See P. A. Fahy, "Some Political Behaviour Patterns and Attitudes of Roman Catholic Priests in a Rural Part of Northern Ireland," *Economic and Social Review* (Dublin), vol. 3, no. 1 (1971), and D. J. D. Roche, W. D. Birrell and J. E. Greer, "A Socio-Political Opinion Profile of Clergymen in Northern Ireland," *Social Studies* (Dublin), vol. 4, no. 2 (1975), pp. 143-51.

prepared to avoid symbolically asserting their long-term aspirations for Irish unity in order to seek immediate gains within a United Kingdom context. During a short period of intense activity from summer 1968 through mid-1969, the movement's main achievements were fourfold. First, civil rights activities established a new form of political action and a new set of political demands within the Catholic community. Second, they served as a recruitment device, bringing forward a new generation of political activists, most of them young university graduates with broader perspectives, both nationally and internationally, than traditional Republicans. Third, the civil rights pressures led the British Labour government to press Terence O'Neill's Stormont government to introduce changes, and a few tentative steps were taken to neutralize traditional sources of grievance. Fourth and equally important, the novel challenge presented by the civil rights campaign led to divisions among Protestants about how to respond, which culminated in the disruption of the Unionist government itself.

The civil rights campaign is better described as a movement than as an organization. Its activities were the product of local action groups in Belfast, Derry, Tyrone, and elsewhere. It drew together, in temporary alliance, individuals with many different political backgrounds, ranging from Republicans to a few Protestants. Its effective life was short. The first concessions from the O'Neill government were enough to make some give up demonstrations, whereas others pressed relentlessly on. When the February 1969 Stormont election was called, the movement's active members divided, some standing as candidates and others abstaining from party activity. When eight people were killed in the Troubles of August 1969, the nonviolent platform of the civil rights campaign became untenable, temporarily at least. Subsequently, Catholics who had once participated in the civil rights movement (and those who came after them) channelled their activities either into party politics or into Republican organizations including the IRA.

**The SDLP.** The Social Democratic and Labour party was founded in 1970 by a group of ex-civil rights activists who had been elected to Stormont in 1969. Gerry Fitt, a Stormont M.P. from Belfast since 1962 and a Westminster M.P. since 1966, was elected the party's leader. Other founding members included John Hume and Ivan Cooper of Londonderry, Austin Currie of Tyrone, Paddy Devlin of Belfast, and Paddy O'Hanlon of Armagh. Notwithstanding their differences, the founding members were anxious to offer Catholics an organized opposition and one prepared to work within a constitutional framework by means regarded as normal in Britain and America.

In its constitution the SDLP identifies three *immediate* objectives that it wishes to achieve in government: the abolition of discrimination, public ownership of essential industries, and the promotion of employment by state-sponsored industries. These proposals reflect the party's desire to place itself in the mainstream of Western European social democratic parties. The party is also pledged to two *long-term* ideals: socialism and "the cause of Irish unity based on the consent of the majority of people in Northern Ireland." The socialist label is not universally accepted within the party; the lengthy compound name of the SDLP provides an umbrella under which people with a variety of economic views can be accommodated. The party has allowed for but not attracted trade unions to affiliate as organizations, a practice common in the British and Irish Labour parties. The SDLP's commitment to Irish unity is also a source of controversy within and outside the party. Effectively, the aspiration to Irish unity limits the party's appeal to Catholics, although the party is nonsectarian and nominated two Protestants successfully for seats in the 1975 Convention. Within the Catholic community, the SDLP differs from conventional Republican groups because it makes Irish unity conditional upon the consent of the majority, rather than absolute, a right that no portion of the population may deny. While the unity ideal is a link with the Nationalists, the party's emphasis upon social programs and its readiness to work within United Kingdom institutions, both in London and in the Province, differentiates it from the Nationalists.

In the 1973 Assembly election, the SDLP showed that it had a better claim to speak for the Catholic minority than any of the Unionist parties had to speak for the Protestant community as a whole. The SDLP won nineteen seats, against none for the Republicans and the Nationalists. The SDLP took 22 percent of the total vote, against 3 percent for traditional Republican and Nationalist candidates.

The exceptional ground rules laid down for forming a government out of the Assembly made "power sharing" mandatory; the Northern Ireland Constitution Act specified: "executive powers will not be concentrated in elected representatives from one community only." [18] Because it held a monopoly claim to Catholic representation, the SDLP was effectively in a position to veto the formation of any

---

18 *Northern Ireland Constitutional Proposals* (London: Her Majesty's Stationery Office, Cmnd. 5259, 1973), p. 14.

power-sharing Executive it found unacceptable. The SDLP is unique in Ulster politics in that it is the only party representative of Catholics to hold office in Northern Ireland. It formed a power-sharing coalition in January 1974 with Brian Faulkner, then leader of the Unionist party, as head and Gerry Fitt as deputy leader. It did this only after extracting from reluctant Unionists as well as from the British government the Sunningdale agreement which gave institutional form to an "Irish dimension" in Northern Ireland politics. In five months the Executive collapsed, after the resignation of its Unionist members in the face of the Ulster Workers' Council strike. The SDLP could not carry on in a government in which a majority of the majority did not wish to participate.

The collapse of the power-sharing Executive did not alter the SDLP's political objectives, but it greatly affected the climate in which the party advanced its demands. The British government's commitment to power sharing was called into question, and Protestant opposition to any coalition government that Westminster imposed upon an elected Ulster assembly was strengthened. (The SDLP's socialist bias, which might in other countries be controversial, has been largely ignored.) Spokesmen of the Protestant majority have questioned the SDLP's right to impose, as they see it, their principles upon a popularly elected Ulster body. While continuing to look to the British government to guarantee a constitution for the Province, the SDLP does not pledge allegiance to Britain alone, but remains committed in principle to an Irish ideal. The Convention election was intended to discover what compromise, if any, could be reached between mutually incompatible views of power sharing. Gerry Fitt warned that his party would not accept exclusion from power, as the Nationalists had in the past.

> If one section of this House—the minority voice—is excluded, it must be quite obvious to all concerned that there cannot be any hope of peace within this community. No army in the world, however well equipped, will be able to keep the voice of that minority silent.[19]

**The Use of Arms.** The revival of armed Catholic political activity began in the aftermath of the August 1969 Troubles. Catholics interpreted the violence as reflecting the inability or unwillingness of the

---

[19] Statement in *Report of Debates* (Belfast: Her Majesty's Stationery Office, Northern Ireland Constitutional Convention, 28 May 1975), Cols. 48-49.

RUC to protect Catholic areas or restrain Protestants.[20] Moribund Republican organizations had little hardware to contribute on short notice for defensive purposes: revolvers and pre-1914 rifles and shotguns were among the weapons Catholics in Belfast mustered when they feared that a Protestant-led pogrom was imminent. The British army's presence provided a lull—but Ulster Catholics did not regard this as a permanent peace-keeping institution.

*Community defense.* Fear of a Protestant attack stimulated Catholics to organize local defense groups using the parish as the basic unit of organization, a pattern that can be traced back to the eighteenth century. In Belfast, for example, a network of parish defense groups joined together in the Central Citizens' Defence Committee, whose membership included prominent clerics, Catholic laymen, and a few well-known Republicans. The activities of defense committees, like those of their Protestant counterparts, were focused upon the immediate security of their own environs: street patrols, manning barricades, and, for some, drill in the use of arms, either within the parish or at special camps established over the border in the Republic of Ireland. In this confused period, it would be difficult to say whether concerned Catholics were using Republican contacts to supply arms, or whether Republicans were using Catholic concern as the basis for securing support and bases of operations within the Catholic community.

*Attack.* The 1969 Troubles found the Republican movement badly divided about strategy. One faction wished the movement to "go political" in two senses: to concentrate its attention upon plans for a socialist Ireland and to make election campaigning its prime channel of influence. This group, known as the Official Sinn Fein, became dominant in the late 1960s. It has offices in Gardiner Place, Dublin, and it is connected with the Official IRA. The faction wishing to "leave politics aside" and to concentrate on the traditional IRA demand for the independence of the thirty-two counties from Britain withdrew to form its own Republican institutions, known as the Provisional Sinn Fein, with offices in Kevin Street. Its military counterpart is the Provisional IRA, familiarly known as the Provos. The Provos have been more aggressive in their military policy, favoring

---

[20] The Protestant and police interpretation of these events is very different. They perceived the August 1969 Troubles as a Republican-inspired rebellion and took steps to suppress it by attacking its locus, that is, Catholic communities. For an exhaustive account of these events, see *Violence and Civil Disturbances in Northern Ireland in 1969* (Scarman Tribunal Report) (Belfast: Her Majesty's Stationery Office, Cmnd. 566, 1972).

confrontation with and attack upon British troops, in the belief this would hasten the creation of a united Ireland.

The Official IRA issued a truce statement on 29 May 1972, asserting that it wished to see an end to military action by all sides in Northern Ireland, though reserving the right to use force to defend areas attacked by Protestants or the British military. Since then the Provisionals have been the primary rebel force operating in the Province. In late June 1972, the Provisionals announced a truce. The British secretary of state met with the leader of the Provisional IRA Army Council, Sean MacStiofain, to discuss a possible political settlement. The IRA demanded a British declaration of intent to withdraw all forces from Irish soil, a general amnesty for all political prisoners and internees, and a declaration that the future of Northern Ireland was to be decided by the residents of the thirty-two counties of Ireland. The British government refused to accept these terms, and the truce broke down on 9 July. Another truce was announced in February 1975. This truce has lasted longer, but it has also been bloodier. (See Chapter 6.)

Both wings of the IRA [21] agree about several basic aims: the withdrawal of British troops from Ireland, the legalization of all forms of Republican political activity within Northern Ireland, and, eventually, the establishment of a thirty-two-county Irish Republic. They also agree in rejecting the claim of the Irish government in Dublin to be the legitimate government of Ireland, since it has given de facto acceptance to the partition of the island. The IRA carries forward the views of the losing side in the Irish civil war of the early 1920s. And both wings are prepared to use the same types of military tactics such as sniping at British soldiers and RUC men on patrol, setting booby traps and bombs around military-type targets, placing bombs in public places designed to cause maximum panic and terror, and, upon occasion, mounting assassination efforts directed at Protestants or within the Catholic community. The IRA has had greater success in destroying public order in Northern Ireland than in achieving its positive political aims.

The Official and Provisional units of the IRA do not have a monopoly upon attacking British soldiers, policemen, or Protestants in Northern Ireland. The fissiparous character of Republican politics and the need to work in small groups for security reasons make it easy for breakaway groups to form. Moreover, the discipline and chain of

---

[21] The Republicans operate through an army, the IRA, rather than through "paramilitary" organizations, like their Protestant counterparts. The distinction reflects a longer tradition, greater discipline, and greater clarity of aims on the Catholic side.

communication of the Dublin-based Army Council of the Official and Provisional organizations is only imperfectly effective in Northern Ireland. Groups who wish to disobey an order can find many reasons to do so. Alternatively, they can form yet another Republican group. In December 1974, for example, the formation of an Irish Republican Socialist party (IRSP) was announced in Belfast. It claimed to be more truly socialist and actively militant than the Official IRA from which it is a splinter organization. Bernadette Devlin McAliskey, formerly a civil rights member of Parliament at Westminster, is its most prominent supporter. The IRSP also announced that it had a "protector" group, the People's Liberation army. The announcement of this split was followed by internecine war between the Official IRA and the IRSP, with members of each group shot dead in carefully planned assassinations in Belfast.

## The "Extreme" Moderates

Political parties that have sought to draw votes across the sectarian divide have won very limited electoral support. In the Ulster context, their rejection of the use of violence to resolve political conflict and their attempt to unite Protestants and Catholics in political action, though moderate elsewhere, are equally extreme. Certainly, the "extreme" moderates are not a simple compromise between the IRA and the UVF.

**Alliance Party.** The Alliance party was founded in April 1970 as an offshoot of the New Ulster Movement, a biconfessional pressure group that had sought to mobilize middle-of-the-road opinion in favor of reform by conventional methods—issuing press statements, holding meetings, lobbying ministers, and supporting O'Neill in his efforts to reduce tensions. It accepts union with Great Britain as being in the best interests of all Ulstermen, thus aligning itself with Unionist parties. Its emphasis upon antidiscrimination measures and participation by persons from both communities in the government of Ulster is consistent with SDLP statements. Alliance also emphasizes the importance of policing, the enforcement of the law equally against both Protestants and Catholics, and the guarantee of justice to all citizens regardless of religion. This approach combines the Protestants' concern with law and order and the Catholics' concern with equity between religions. Like the Liberal party in England, Alliance rejects commitment to a socialist or a conservative economic philosophy. The party accepts the religious-national divide as *the* issue in Ulster politics. It is distinctive in that it tries to bring together people from both sides of the divide in a biconfessional party, rather than campaign solely within one community—or pretend that the divide does not exist. The Alliance party's first parliamentary representatives came to it from previous positions in the Unionist and Nationalist parties at Stormont. Of the eight Alliance candidates successful in the 1973 Assembly election, six were entering office for the first time as Alliance men and two had previously sought election in 1969 as unofficial pro-O'Neill Unionists. The party has consistently nominated both Protestant and Catholic candidates in local and provincial elections. Only one of its Catholic candidates, Oliver Napier, was successful in 1973. He became the Alliance leader in the short-lived power-sharing Executive. In the February 1974 Westminster election, Alliance nominated three candidates and won 3 percent of the vote; in October, it nominated five candidates and won 6 percent of the vote.

**Northern Ireland Labour Party (NILP).** For generations the Northern Ireland Labour party and its predecessors regarded the border question as of little importance and remained neutral on whether Northern Ireland should be part of the United Kingdom or the Republic. According to the NILP, economic issues were the most important questions facing Ulstermen. In 1949, however, the NILP finally came down in favor of the United Kingdom link—and its ranks promptly split. In the 1958 and 1962 Stormont elections the NILP won four seats. But the prosperity associated with the early years of O'Neill Unionism slowed its growth among Protestants, and the challenge of the civil rights movement, which the NILP was hesitant to endorse, lost it Catholic support. The party's claim to be the sole spokesman for the British Labour party in Northern Ireland has been eroded by the rise of the SDLP, which has friends in London among British Labour politicians who favor a united Ireland. As the Troubles have intensified, the Northern Ireland Labour party has lost traditional Protestant working-class support in Belfast to Loyalist organizations. In the 1973 Assembly election, it won only a single seat and took less than 3 percent of the vote. The one NILP man elected, David Bleakley, had made his commitment to Unionism as well as socialism clear by accepting a temporary post in Brian Faulkner's Unionist cabinet in 1971. Other former members of the NILP are active today in the Republican movement, the SDLP, and Loyalist paramilitary organizations.

**The British Role**

The British government has become an increasingly important party to the Ulster Troubles since the occurrences of 1969. Prior to that time, London had no direct involvement in the most important political affairs of the Province, and Ulster questions were normally not allowed to be debated at Westminster. The Labour government of Harold Wilson sought to encourage Terence O'Neill to accelerate the pace of reform—but the result was not sufficient to satisfy Catholics. In August 1969, the British government sent in more than 10,000 troops to maintain order. Since that time, the army has been the largest single full-time security force in the Province. While the Labour government sympathized with the Catholics, its troops were used in support of the Protestant Stormont government.[22] The use of the army to carry out internment in August 1971 and the army's responsibility for the repeated "screening" (or harassment) of Catholics suspected of Republican sympathies and for deaths such as those of thirteen young Catholic men shot in Londonderry on Bloody Sunday, 1972, has made it unpopular among many elements of the Catholic population. The hesitancy of the army to patrol in "no go" areas dominated by the IRA has attracted Protestant criticism. This has intensified as the army's efforts to end IRA violence have failed. The army nonetheless remains the major barrier between Catholic and Protestant paramilitary groups who, in the absence of British forces, might turn intermittent guerrilla attacks into all-out civil war.

**Direct Rule.** British ministers have had political responsibility for governing Northern Ireland since March 1972, when the old Stormont administration was abolished.[23] A secretary of state for Northern Ireland (currently Merlyn Rees) exercises nearly all formal powers except for those vested in the Ministry of Defence, the Treasury, or other agencies responsible for major government functions throughout the United Kingdom. The creation of the power-sharing Executive was a result of the persistent cajoling of the first secretary of state, William Whitelaw. During its operation, the British government remained responsible for security.

The limits of British power were revealed by the Ulster Workers' Council strike in May 1974. The British government refused to negotiate with the strikers, and it refused to use troops in an effort to end a strike intended to destroy the London-sponsored government of the moment. The strikers won. The credibility of British power was greatly reduced within Northern Ireland. In London, the will to gov-

---

22 See L. J. Callaghan, *A House Divided* (London: Collins, 1973). Callaghan was the minister in charge of Ulster affairs in 1969.

23 For an account of the workings of the Northern Ireland Office, see Lord Windlesham, "Ministers in Ulster," *Public Administration*, vol. 51 (Autumn 1973).

ern Ulster also sank. Yet Britain once again had to assume this responsibility.

The Northern Ireland Office (NIO) claims authority in Northern Ireland by virtue of a British act of Parliament. This is both its strength and its weakness. The NIO can claim to be independent of Protestant-Catholic conflicts in Ulster, because it is responsible to a Westminster Parliament that is dominated by parties organized without regard to religion. By the same token, it is not responsible to an Ulster electorate, for there are only 12 Ulster representatives among the 635 M.P.s at Westminster. Neither Protestants nor Catholics can have confidence that the actions of the Westminster-controlled NIO will be consistent with the views of a majority of Ulstermen. British pressure has led to the downfall of three successive Unionist leaders: London asked them to do what a majority at Westminster wanted and this proved to be unacceptable to a majority of their Ulster supporters. The transfer of Stormont powers to Westminster is particularly troublesome to Loyalists. A 1949 British act of Parliament required a positive vote of the predominantly Protestant Stormont Parliament before any measures could be taken leading to the unification of Ireland. By suspending Stormont, the British government took from Ulster Protestants what they regarded as their only lawful surety against a possible sell-out by Britain to Dublin. Protestant paramilitants have capitalized upon the resulting anxiety; they have recruited and drilled men in the belief that such a force could be used if Britain ever sought to placate pro-Irish groups by handing the Province over to Dublin.

**Security.** Initially British politicians believed that the most important power of government in Northern Ireland, as in England, was the power to spend money to bring benefits to the citizens of the Province, such as new homes, improved social services, greater investment in public services, and employment maintained by government grants to industry.[24] The large sums of money poured into Northern Ireland in efforts to "buy" support have not been sufficient to secure the unconditional allegiance of Ulstermen to the government that pays for its welfare and economic benefits.

British politicians soon learned that "real" politics in Ulster (as against "normal" politics in England) is about security and public

---

[24] For a British tabulation of finance, see Northern Ireland Office, *Finance and the Economy* (London: Her Majesty's Stationery Office, 1974). For varied comments, see *Ulster: The Economic Case* (Belfast: Ulster Television Publications, 1975).

order. This is the first responsibility of any institution that claims to be governing a territory anywhere in the modern world. In most societies, order can be taken for granted, but not in Northern Ireland. In pursuit of order, British-led security forces have dispensed with the conventional rules of law recognized for centuries in English and American courts: the right of habeas corpus, the calling and cross-examination of witness, and the proferring against the accused of a specific charge or sentence for a criminal act. Such departures from conventional legal standards are customary in Ireland where, in the centuries of English involvement, English-type statutes have rarely been relied upon exclusively. The test of a policy designed to create public order in the midst of internal war is not whether it conforms to conventional liberal assumptions, but whether it produces order.

Four security forces are operating in Northern Ireland under the authority of the British government. Only the army itself is manned by British personnel recruited primarily in Great Britain and rotated in and out of the Province as the security situation makes appropriate, in numbers ranging from 10,000 to 22,000 since the start of internment in 1971. The great bulk of the army is not deployed on the border, defending Ulster from external attack from the Irish Republic, but rather within the Province, defending communal ghettos from attack by the other side or patrolling and policing within neighborhoods. The more contact the army has with Ulstermen, the more effective it can be in arresting paramilitants and seizing arms and ammunition. By the same token, the greater the potential friction between the army and the Catholics or Protestants it is policing, the greater the risk of its being attacked. Since 1969, 246 British soldiers have been killed in Ulster, almost all by Republican gunmen or bombs. The army's losses have been greater than in colonial-type policing in Palestine, Cyprus, or Kenya. Only the Korean War and a thirteen-year security operation in Malaya have cost the British army more lives since 1945.

The British army is relieved of tedious patrol duties by the part-time Ulster Defence Regiment, a fully armed locally raised force of 7,700 men. The UDR's functions resemble those of the old B Specials; it differs in being under British army command rather than under the command of Stormont politicians. The conflict between Catholics and the British army has led to a diminution of Catholic participation in the UDR, from an initial high of 18 percent in 1970 to 3 percent by spring 1975. The army claims it carefully screens all UDR applicants to guard against infiltration by paramilitary groups, but Catholic politicians cite instances in which the UDR's own security procedures have failed, and its own members or ex-members have been charged with crimes.

The Royal Ulster Constabulary has grown in numerical strength in the course of the Troubles, but its effective peace-keeping role has declined. First, the British army has taken over responsibility for maintaining order in the streets. Second, the army has become active in seeking out and apprehending persons suspected of rebellious activities. Internment and the creation of special courts have changed the definition of security work, which is no longer a matter of arresting individuals on charges of specified criminal acts, but of detaining individuals suspected of being threats to the security of the state.[25] Furthermore, the RUC's present size, 4,800 men (1,700 below authorized strength), is inadequate to contain violence, given the level currently found in Northern Ireland. Fourth among security forces is an RUC Reserve of 4,900 part-time policemen, but this force is little concerned with serious political security work and is 2,000 below its authorized strength. The RUC and even more the RUC Reserve are overwhelmingly Protestant. Before the Troubles, Catholics constituted about 10 percent of the force. The IRA campaign of assassination aimed against the police has not encouraged Catholics to increase their proportion in the RUC.

The aims of the British government are multiple. One is to secure "violence reduced to an acceptable level," a phrase used by Reginald Maudling when, as a British cabinet minister, he was responsible for Ulster security.[26] Containing violence is the responsibility of security forces directed by professional soldiers, but final political responsibility rests with the secretary of state for defence in London. The inclination of professional security officers is to identify actual or potential creators of disorder and imprison them, and the powers of internment and detention that they have been granted place few legal obstacles in their way. For years security officials have been promising that "acceptable conditions" are just around the corner. But such statements beg the question: acceptable to whom? Englishmen and Dubliners have shown a very low tolerance for IRA or Protestant-inspired violence. For example, following the Birmingham pub bombings of November 1974, it took Westminster just one day to pass a Prevention of Terrorism Act that gave the government powers to detain or restrict to one part of the United Kingdom citizens who,

[25] For a critical comparison of British army and RUC security methods, see Boyle, Hadden, and Hillyard, *Law and State.*
[26] The remark was made in December 1971, four months after the introduction of internment. See Sunday Times Insight Team, *Ulster*, p. 309.

everywhere else in the Western world, enjoy freedom of movement within their own country. In the first six months of 1975, British discussions with the Provisional IRA resulted in a truce of sorts. Only one soldier died in this period. But this has not earned Britain the gratitude of Ulstermen, for in the same period ninety-eight Ulstermen died. Such a level of violence is not acceptable to those who suffer its effects firsthand.

**The Restoration of Civil Government.** A second goal of the British government is to restore civil government in Northern Ireland. This is the principal concern of the Northern Ireland Office, which, in conjunction with Northern Ireland civil servants, is responsible for the day-to-day administration of the machinery of government in the Province. Successive British politicians have reckoned that to restore civil government requires the consent and cooperation of Ulstermen. In pursuit of this aim, the British government was prepared to undertake truce negotiations with the IRA in 1972 and again in 1974–75. It has not been anxious to negotiate with Protestant paramilitants, but does so from time to time. In effect, it has left control of those forces to the RUC, thus avoiding the prospect of a British army-Protestant paramilitary confrontation that would result in a "two-front" war unwanted by the Ministry of Defence. A violent challenge to British troops is not desired by Ulster Protestants; their paramilitants prefer to attack Catholics. But the efforts of Northern Ireland secretaries to move toward a restoration of civil government have been obstructed by the short-term security concerns that tend to preempt the attention of all parties to the dispute. When the guns are out, there is a limit to what elected politicians can do.

Successive Labour and Conservative efforts to govern Northern Ireland, whether by direct rule or through formal and informal pressures upon locally elected assemblies, have achieved consensus within the British House of Commons about what ought to be done in Ulster. But these efforts have not restored civil government within Northern Ireland. Westminster endorsement may be a necessary condition for establishing a durable constitution in Ulster, but it is not a sufficient condition. No constitution can be established in Northern Ireland that is not acceptable to the bulk of the parties to the dispute. Some British politicians have begun to wonder since the 1974 UWC strike whether the only consensus possible in Ulster may be negative: a vote of no confidence in the continuance of British direct rule. If this is true, the best contribution Britain might make to Northern Ireland would be to leave it. On the occasions when the Westminster consensus has been broken, the impetus has come as often from advocates of "pulling out" as from M.P.s who wish to make greater effort to maintain the United Kingdom as it is.

## Ulster and the Republic

The policy of the Republic of Ireland toward Ulster is complex and ambiguous. Article 2 of its constitution states: "The national territory consists of the whole island of Ireland, its islands and the territorial seas." Anyone born in Northern Ireland may claim citizenship in the Republic and some Ulster Catholics, including M.P.s, do. Under British law, they do not thereby lose their British citizenship, nor do they lose the right to be elected to Stormont or to the Westminster Parliament. In many ways the Republic gives de facto recognition to Northern Ireland's position within the United Kingdom, most notably by meetings with the head of the old Stormont government in the days of Terence O'Neill, and by public and private representations to the British government in London, the de facto sovereign authority. Moreover, international organizations to which both Britain and Ireland belong, such as the United Nations and the European Economic Community, recognize Northern Ireland as part of the United Kingdom, not as part of the Republic.

In the half-century since 1921, the Dublin regime and Northern Ireland have evolved in different ways. The leaders of the Republic initially sought to develop their society in terms of Catholic, Gaelic, and agrarian ideals. In Northern Ireland, by contrast, the industrial area around Belfast has continued to dominate, and the benefits of industrialism, including the social services of the modern welfare state, have been provided under British sponsorship. Politics in the North has been about very different issues than in the South. In the North, a Catholic minority of one-third was uncertainly loyal to the regime. In the South, a much smaller Protestant minority—one in twenty—gave unconditional allegiance to the Republic. In consequence, by the time the Troubles started, opinion surveys showed that Protestant and Catholic Ulstermen thought that they had more in common with each other than they had with their coreligionists from Ireland or Britain.[27]

The Republican movement is the only element anywhere in Ireland actively seeking the unity of the thirty-two counties. Because the IRA opposes the Dublin regime, which acquiesced in the partition

---

[27] See Rose, *Governing without Consensus*, p. 214.

of Ireland in 1921, the Dublin government has from time to time been the object of violent Republican attacks and has used security forces harshly against Republican organizations. Although the IRA is illegal in the Republic, it operates there through front organizations or clandestinely, a fact well known to Ulster Protestants. Moreover, the IRA's desire for Irish unity, however much its means may differ from those of the Dublin government, is consistent with the goal to which the Irish government too is committed.

The outbreak of killing in August 1969 immediately brought to life the Republic's dormant commitment to a united Ireland. Catholics in the South sympathized with their coreligionists in Northern Ireland. Moreover, Ulster Catholics looked to the Republic for many things: a haven for families burnt out of homes, political influence in London, Washington, and the U.N., and, last and not always least, arms and assistance for "self-defense" measures. Officials of the Dublin government began assisting Northern Catholic groups to gain arms training in the South and to buy arms on the Continent with government funds. Two members of the cabinet of Jack Lynch were forced to resign and were indicted for participating in arms deals, along with military intelligence officers. The individuals charged were tried and acquitted in 1970. The evidence made clear that the Dublin government had given military aid to Northern Catholics but left unclear which individuals had been responsible for such action.

The Irish government's influence upon Ulster security is indirect but not insignificant. The Irish army of about 12,800 is a negligible force, politically and militarily. It is smaller than the UDR, the RUC, and the RUC Reserve together, and little better armed. Moreover, the Irish army is a defensive force. It is not organized to conduct border operations as are armies, legal or liberationist, in the Middle East. The Irish police (*Garda Siochanna*) is more significant, for its actions determine the extent to which Republicans may operate more or less without harassment in the Republic. Laws give the *Garda* less freedom of action than the British army has in Northern Ireland. Nonetheless, special courts and laws permit persons arrested and charged with belonging to the IRA to be jailed. Irish laws do not, however, permit the extradition to Northern Ireland of persons accused of political crimes or crimes connected with political offenses, for example murder or robbery carried out in the name of the Republican cause. Ulster Protestants complain that the Irish police are soft on Republicans— just as Ulster Catholics complain that the RUC is soft on Protestant paramilitants. To protest against this softness, Protestant paramilitants have carried out occasional attacks on Catholics in border counties of the Republic and one major bombing in Dublin which killed twenty-six people.

While the theoretical ideal of the Dublin government remains a united Ireland, its practical goals are much less ambitious. In positive terms, Dublin would like to see the formation of a Northern Ireland government in which power was shared by Protestants and Catholics. It would hope that such a government would gradually increase cross-border contacts with Dublin. In unspecified and distant ways this could gradually lead to the unification of Ireland. If forced to choose, the Dublin government would rather stabilize government within Northern Ireland than promote Irish unity. One reason for this is a desire to accommodate the immediate interests of Northern Catholics. Another is the Republic's immediate interest in securing peace on its own borders and avoiding the risk of the political violence in Ulster spreading into the twenty-six counties. Violence could spread if the Dublin government attempted to crack down on the IRA which then attacked its southern as well as its northern enemy. Violence in the Republic could also come as a by-product of massive Protestant-Catholic fighting in the North, drawing in southern sympathizers (the so-called Doomsday scenario), or it could be brought south by Ulster Protestant paramilitants. The minimum goal of the Dublin government is to maintain the twenty-six counties free of the political violence that is racking six counties of Ulster.

From time to time, references to other nations appear in discussions of Northern Ireland, but these are of little consequence. Its small size and the absence of valuable raw materials make Ulster an unlikely attraction for a power not already involved there. Any informed reconnaissance of the situation would make evident that any external group would soon get bogged down in the complexities of local conflicts. For example, Communist politics in Northern Ireland is defined not only in terms of a Moscow-Maoist division, but also by a Protestant-Catholic division. Some Protestant paramilitant and IRA groups have contained elements with Marxist or Communist outlooks—but their political significance has always derived from their religious affiliation first and foremost. The U.S. Department of State has consistently sought to remain aloof from the troubles affecting two nations with which it has close ties. Individual congressmen have from time to time voiced sympathies with one side or another,.according to personal predilection and constituency pressures. The most significant American (and Canadian) contribution appears to be money raised for "defense" and assistance in procuring and shipping arms. Such aid appears to have been provided to both Catholics and Protestants, but to have helped the Republicans more, given the larger number of recent Irish Catholic immigrants to North America. Probably the outsiders who have benefitted most from the Troubles have been dealers and brokers in arms from Hamburg to Libya. To continue to benefit, however, they must maintain their distance. Otherwise, they too will find themselves tagged as Protestant or Catholic arms dealers, whether they are actually Christian, Muslim, or atheist.

## Strange Bedfellows

Because Ulstermen differ about both the ends of politics (unity with the Republic of Ireland or loyalty to Britain) and the means (resolving disputes by the ballot or by all measures necessary), politics in Ulster, even more than in other lands, can make for strange bedfellows. Ulstermen who give first priority to resolving disputes at the ballot box are grouped together as parliamentary politicians, a category embracing everyone from Ian Paisley's Democratic Unionists through the Alliance party to the SDLP. Protestant and Catholic paramilitary organizations sometimes meet to discuss matters of common concern, such as their shared rejection of the authority of the current British and Irish regimes, or their opposition to internment regulations. Ulstermen who give first priority to the maintenance of Protestant rule may find themselves working with any number of paramilitary organizations, as well as with elected officeholders from the main Loyalist parties. Similarly, Ulstermen with aspirations for a united Ireland may encourage both the SDLP and the IRA to work to such an end, albeit by different means. Organizations disagreeing about many things may find that they draw support from the same community—and sometimes from the same families or individuals.

The extreme developments that confront Ulstermen—mass internment, deaths by the dozen in concerted terrorist attacks, the suspension of duly elected governments or their resignation in the face of intimidation—challenge the survival of every political organization described in this chapter. The ambivalence of Ulstermen toward political means and ends makes it difficult for organizations to predict how their nominal followers will react. Thus it is hardly surprising that of the seven major parties described in this chapter, only two, the Official Unionists and the Northern Ireland Labour party, were formed before 1970—and both of these organizations have had histories of recurring splits. Equally, of the various types of paramilitary and military organizations described in this chapter, none existed in its present form before the Troubles began and all have been plagued by splits and threats of division within their ranks.

The party system in Northern Ireland today is different from that in any other Western nation. It more nearly resembles the party system of a Latin American country, where military and foreign involvement in politics are taken for granted, or that of Weimar Germany or the first Austrian Republic between the wars when armed groups competed with parties for the power to rule. These comparisons are a reminder that, while armed groups can destroy electoral parties or even a regime, they cannot of themselves constitute civil government. Civil government requires not only the authority that comes from force, but also the force that comes from political authority.

# 4

# CAMPAIGNING FOR
# A CONSTITUTION

*The people of Northern Ireland must play a crucial part
in determining their own future. No political structure can
endure without their support.*

British Government White Paper, July 1974

In a parliamentary election in Britain, the party that wins the most
votes expects to take all the power. The defeated party accepts the
rules of the game, because it expects to enjoy the same advantage at
a later date when its own efforts or the defects of the government of
the day will return it to office. In Northern Ireland, there has never
been a simple alternation of office between "ins" and "outs" because,
in the words of one scholar, "there is no floating vote on the constitutional issue."[1]

## The Circumstances of the Election

Electing a constitutional convention is fundamentally different from
electing a government. Delegates to a constitutional convention have
the task of deciding both the name of the game and its rules. Americans assume that this presents no problem, given the success of the
eighteenth-century Philadelphia convention in creating a union from
a confederation of states and devising a novel instrument of government that has lasted for two centuries. Moreover, many American
states have rewritten their constitutions with little public or political
controversy. But Ulstermen lack the basic consensus of Americans
about the boundaries of their country and the manner in which it

---

[1] J. L. McCracken, quoted in Rose, *Governing without Consensus*, p. 218.

should be governed. A gathering of Ulstermen asked to establish a government of their Province—if they are at all representative of the Ulster people—is far more likely to produce arguments about ends and means than consensus.

**A Change of Policy.** Notwithstanding dissension within the Province, the election of a Northern Ireland Constitutional Convention did take place, for the British government concluded, after the UWC strike of May 1974, that it could not govern Northern Ireland without taking the views of Ulstermen into account.[2] This was a reversal of the policy begun in August 1969 of attempting to "neutralize" government by withdrawing powers from elected Ulstermen. The policy was initiated in Londonderry in November 1968. The Protestant-dominated council, holding power through gerrymandering, was suspended. It was not replaced by a council elected according to the principle of "one man, one vote, one value," which would have given Catholics responsibility for local government. It was replaced instead by a development corporation appointed by the Unionist government at Stormont. Subsequent measures to neutralize government have included: reduction in the number of local government units and the removal of many of their powers to boards appointed centrally by Stormont; creation of an appointed Northern Ireland Housing Executive to exercise housing responsibilities formerly vested in locally elected councils; appointment of a civil servant as ombudsman to investigate, subject to severe restrictions, complaints of maladministration; effective transfer of both police and public order responsibilities from Stormont to British hands; and, finally and most emphatically, suspension of the Stormont Parliament in March 1972—followed two years later by the suspension of the British-sponsored Northern Ireland Assembly.

British officials have made only token efforts to associate representative Ulstermen with appointed bodies. Instead, they have sought persons who, in addition to having professional qualifications as lawyers, businessmen, or trade unionists, were "nonpolitical." Of the eleven Ulstermen appointed to the Advisory Commission of the Northern Ireland Office established after direct rule was introduced in 1972, eight had confined their public activities to nonrepresentative (that is, nonelectoral) politics.

[2] For the Northern Ireland Office account of reasons leading up to the calling of a convention, see *The Northern Ireland Constitution* (London: Her Majesty's Stationery Office, Cmnd. 5675, 1974) and *Government of Northern Ireland* (London: Her Majesty's Stationery Office, Discussion Paper No. 3, 1975).

Each reform measure was justified at the time of its adoption as a step toward good government, or at least as a step away from bad government. For example, the creation of a single Northern Ireland Housing Executive in place of many housing authorities controlled by small elected local councils was said to rationalize housing through economies of scale—and to remove opportunities for personal patronage and/or religious discrimination in local housing allocation. The removal of local government powers especially affronted Protestant politicians, who had controlled most local government bodies previous to British intervention. The removal of security responsibility from Stormont to Westminster meant that Catholics turned their criticism from the Stormont-led RUC to the British army, which they had no power to influence. Protestants criticized the British government too, when British security measures failed to end the IRA attacks. The suspension of Stormont and the Assembly left the British-directed administration free from responsibility to an Ulster assembly, while the politicians elected to these bodies continued to be asked by their quondam constituents to look after their interests.

British policy since 1969 has been based on the assumption that the British government is itself a "neutral" force, because it is outside the traditional enmities of the Province. British officials have downplayed their Britishness since only one community in the Province identifies with Britain. This gesture gives little assurance to Catholics, while inducing Protestant anxieties. Concurrently, Britain has sought to exercise greater and greater influence upon Ulster affairs. Clear-sighted Ulstermen have not had difficulty in spotting the inconsistencies in this position. Their views of British policy divide according to their perceptions of which side Britain is "neutral against" at any given moment.

The inconsistency of the British position is illustrated by the decision to elect a representative assembly in 1973. Ulstermen were invited to elect representatives for the first time in more than four very troubled years. But there were two catches. The first was that the new Northern Ireland Assembly was not given power over security, the central issue in the life-and-death politics of the Province. The second was that a Northern Ireland government could operate again only after the British secretary of state had approved the composition of the new Northern Ireland Executive, in which, it was stipulated, power had to be shared by two communities. In other words, Ulster people could elect whomever they wished—but they could be governed only by an Executive that had the approval of Westminster. The Executive failed. While it had the confidence of a majority of the

British Parliament, the leaders of the Ulster Workers' Council strike asserted that it lacked the confidence of a majority of Ulster Protestants, and a demoralized British government was unwilling to find out whether the Loyalists had the support they claimed: it refused to agree to the strikers' demand for an immediate general election to test popular support for policies launched under British sponsorship.

The collapse of the power-sharing Executive left the British government with neither wish nor will to govern Northern Ireland indefinitely. All it had was the responsibility. Cabinet ministers could be heard to mutter that the sooner Britain "pulled out"—whatever that vague phrase might mean—the better. In July 1974, a British government White Paper proposed the election of a convention whose task it would be to recommend how the government of Northern Ireland should be constituted. The British government, however, once again emphasized its formal sovereignty over Northern Ireland by laying down three conditions that were to be incorporated in any constitutional proposals emanating from such a convention: (1) power sharing by Protestants and Catholics; (2) an "Irish dimension" recognizing and providing for Ulster's "special relationship with another country, the Republic of Ireland"; and (3) acceptance of the British Parliament's right to decide *whether* the recommendations of Ulstermen were to be enacted as law.[3] The White Paper stated that the British government would play no part in the proceedings of the convention. But by laying down its three conditions, the government gave a very broad hint to Ulstermen which parties they should vote for if they wished to be sure of giving Northern Ireland the kind of government that Britain wanted. While the Northern Ireland Office, as the formal governing authority, undoubtedly had the right to stipulate these conditions, it did not necessarily have the power to realize them. In effect, the White Paper allowed Ulstermen to vote for any representatives they wished in the election to the Northern Ireland Constitutional Convention—but specified what the majority of the delegates, whatever their campaign pledges, would be expected to do on matters of central political concern.

In the nine months between the announcement of plans for a constitutional convention and the announcement of a date for the ballot, Ulstermen fortuitously had yet another chance to express their views: the October 1974 United Kingdom general election. This showed that they had not changed at all. Ten of the twelve Ulster seats at Westminster were won by Loyalist candidates, one by SDLP

---

[3] *The Northern Ireland Constitution*, p. 16.

leader Gerry Fitt, and one by a Republican. The Loyalists polled 58 percent of the vote, and anti-British Republican candidates 8 percent. The parties supporting power sharing took 34 percent of the vote with the SDLP contributing two-thirds of this power-sharing total.

On the security front, there was one major development: negotiations between the British government and the Provisional IRA led to an IRA declaration of truce, initially effective on Christmas 1974 and subsequently confirmed in early February. The statement was immediately followed by a reduction in British army patrolling in Catholic areas. The British secretary of state, Merlyn Rees, announced that he would make the release of internees contingent upon and proportional to evidence of a sustained cessation of violence. The negotiations gave de facto political recognition to the IRA for the British government publicly agreed to work with Provisional Sinn Fein incident centers in efforts to prevent isolated shootings between British soldiers and Republican gunmen from escalating. Protestants feared that, however welcome a truce might be, the negotiations with the Provisionals would bode no good for Protestant political interests. They noted that the Provisional IRA did not abandon its immediate military objectives: a date for the withdrawal of British troops, an amnesty for all political prisoners, whether interned or convicted on charges, and British recognition of the Republican claim that the future of Northern Ireland should be decided on a thirty-two-county basis.

On 25 March 1975 the prime minister of Great Britain, Harold Wilson, made a flying five-hour trip to Belfast and announced that the Convention election would be held on 1 May. This was Wilson's first trip to the troubled Province since his attack on Ulster "spongers" in a T.V. speech during the UWC strike the previous May. Wilson did not indulge in a meet-the-people tour. He moved through Belfast in an armour-plated Jaguar with bulletproof windows and traveled to and from the military airfield by helicopter, with an army marksman warily surveying the scene for signs that the truce might be broken. Wilson concentrated upon meeting politicians, including a self-proclaimed spokesman for the UVF, and church leaders. In the words of a journalist, the announcement of the Convention election showed that the idea of "producing a British-made solution for local politicians to work is dead." [4] But the prime minister, while emphasizing that the Convention would be a forum for Ulstermen, simultaneously stressed that its recommendations required the acceptance of the British Parliament.

---

[4] "Mr. Wilson Names May 1 as Date for Ulster Election," The *Times* (London), 26 March 1975.

**Proportional Representation and the Single Transferable Vote.**
The Convention was the third election held in Northern Ireland in
the 1970s under the single transferable vote (STV) proportional representation (PR) system. This method of casting and counting votes is
very different from the simple plurality election of representatives
from single-member districts employed by the British House of Commons and the United States Congress. It is also very different from
forms of proportional representation employed in continental Europe.
The only Western nation that regularly uses the system is the Republic of Ireland.[5]

The proportional representation element in the electoral system
determines how many candidates of each party are successful. The
Province is divided into twelve constituencies, the same twelve that
send one M.P. each to Westminster. The number of registered electors
in each Westminster constituency varies from 66,000 in the inner city
area of West Belfast to 117,000 in South Antrim, a range also found
in constituencies elsewhere in Britain. Whereas each of these seats,
whatever its size, returns one M.P. to the Parliament at Westminster,
in a PR election the number of seats assigned to each constituency
varies, according to the size of the electorate, from five to eight. A seat
is awarded to any candidate who wins a quota of votes; the quota is
calculated by dividing the total number of seats plus one into the total
number of valid votes cast and then adding one to the result. In other
words, in a constituency of 60,000 votes and five seats, a quota consists of one vote more than one-sixth of the total (10,000 + 1). If
five candidates each gain this total, collectively taking 50,005 votes,
they win the five seats, for the sixth candidate can have won, at most,
only 9,995 votes.

The Northern Ireland proportional representation ballot differs
from those of continental European systems in that a voter casts his
ballot not for a party but for individual candidates in the order of his
preference. The preferences are listed—1, 2, 3, and so on—as far
down the list of candidates as a voter wishes to go. In a constituency
with six seats and eighteen candidates, a voter can express up to
eighteen preferences through his single transferable vote. A candidate
who achieves a surplus of votes above the quota required to win a
seat has his surplus vote transferred in proportion to its size to the
candidates who stand next in preference among his supporters. Once

---

[5] For an account of Irish electoral politics, see Basil Chubb, *The Government and
Politics of Ireland* (Stanford: Stanford University Press, 1970). For the relative
importance of district size and proportional representation, see Douglas Rae,
*The Political Consequences of Electoral Laws* (New Haven: Yale University Press,
1971).

this is done, the candidate with the lowest total of votes is eliminated, and his votes are transferred to those ranking next in the preference of his supporters. An individual can rank all the candidates of one party as his initial preferences, before going on to candidates of his second best party. Alternatively, he can spread his top preferences among candidates of different parties. The decision is up to the elector. An individual voter may stop numbering preferences at any point—for example, after he has run out of "acceptable" Protestants or "acceptable" Catholics whom he is willing to support. Because some voters will not spread their preferences across a wide range of parties, after the final count candidates with the largest number of votes yet short of the quota are declared elected up to the number of seats still unfilled. (For a detailed illustration, see Appendix A.)

The British government did not adopt this intricate form of proportional representation because it had been converted to the merits of assigning representation proportionate to popular support. As recently as 1970 the Unionist government had reiterated, with British endorsement, that a change in the Ulster electoral system could not be considered by the committee reforming local government in Northern Ireland. Nor was Westminster at that time prepared to grant a hearing to proponents of proportional representation in Britain. The adoption of proportional representation in Ulster under British government patronage was a sign of desperation: anything, however un-British it appeared, was worth trying in the attempt to break the impasse facing Westminster following the imposition of direct rule from London in 1972. There was a precedent for employing the system, inasmuch as the STV proportional representation ballot had been required by Westminster when it had initially established the Parliament at Stormont, and this system had been used for the Stormont elections of 1921 and 1925, which the Unionists had won with sweeping majorities. It had then been abolished in favor of the Anglo-American system of simple-plurality single-member seats in the belief that this would strengthen Unionist control of Stormont by making it difficult for Unionist splinter groups to win seats and by encouraging a two-party system. The Nationalists would be a permanent second party that could always be outvoted on straight sectarian lines.[6]

The British government hoped that precisely those characteristics usually described as the evils of proportional representation would prove beneficial in Northern Ireland in the 1970s. In particular, it hoped that PR would eliminate the Unionist monopoly of power by encouraging the proliferation of parties and thus the splitting of the

---

[6] See Mansergh, *Government of Northern Ireland.*

Protestant vote to such an extent that no party, Protestant or otherwise, would win half the seats. Some British officials also expressed the belief that proportional representation would strengthen the so-called moderates, because moderate candidates might attract second preference or "lesser evil" votes from electors in both communities. In any case, the new system could not weaken the moderates because they were already so weak under the old system.

The proportional representation system did not cause a fragmentation of parties in Northern Ireland, for parties were already fragmented before the system was introduced. In the ten elections under the old system, four or five different parties always won representation in the fifty-two-seat Parliament. In a tabulation of the results of the 1969 Stormont election, thirteen different party groupings were recorded—as well as three successful independents.[7] In the two ballots held for the Westminster Parliament in 1974 under British rules, six parties contested seats, counting the three Loyalist groups as a single-party coalition. The multiplicity of parties was an argument in favor of introducing PR, which would allow each to attain representation approximately in proportion to its popular support. This could not happen under the British system. For example, in the February 1974 election, the Loyalists won 51 percent of the vote and 92 percent of the seats. The following October their share of the vote rose to 58 percent, but their share of seats fell to 83 percent.

The introduction of proportional representation provided an incentive to every party to seek its maximum strength, whether this would be more than half the vote in a constituency or as little as 11.12 percent of the vote, enough to win one place in the eight-seat constituency of South Antrim. A party that might reckon to take 15 to 20 percent of the vote and be doomed to the status of a third-party perpetual loser in Britain could contest every multimember constituency in Northern Ireland and expect to stand a good chance of winning at least one seat in each. The electoral system offered parties no incentive to seek votes across the religious divide, because the chances of winning an extra seat by adding a few votes from the other community were much less than the chances of losing votes by appearing "soft" on the issues that were of central concern within the party's home community.

The single transferable vote encourages each candidate to seek the maximum number of first preferences, even at the expense of party colleagues running in the same constituency. The system leaves to the voter rather than to the party organization the choice of which

---

[7] See Rose, *Governing without Consensus*, p. 220.

candidates will receive the one, two, or three seats that the party wins in a constituency. Northern Ireland parties have usually sought to nominate more candidates than they hoped to get elected so as to maximize the number of first-preference votes attracted on personal or parochial grounds. They have also tended to scatter their candidates geographically around the spacious constituencies. Equally, however, parties wish to avoid dividing a more or less fixed quantity of support among too many candidates for fear that all of their candidates might be eliminated because of initially low support. In effect, the STV ballot creates an American-style primary election, which decides which of a party's candidates are preferred by its supporters, within the context of a general election.

## The Competing Parties

The first question that the Convention election prompted was: who would fight? British officials hoped that the Provisional IRA truce would coax Provisional Sinn Fein to seek votes as an alternative to extraconstitutional action. Similarly, they hoped that paramilitary groups and those active in the Ulster Workers' Council might seek votes as an alternative to more immediately threatening forms of influence. In the event, the largest extraconstitutional groups in both communities refused a public test of their strength at the ballot box. Effectively, the election campaign for the Convention developed into a contest between familiar parties along customary Ulster lines: the three Loyalist parties, the UPNI, and the Northern Ireland Labour party battled for the Protestant vote; the SDLP sought to ward off a Republican challenge for the Catholic vote; and the Alliance party battled for whatever votes it could find among those wishing to support a party that explicitly appealed to some elements in both communities.

**The Loyalist Position.** The Loyalist Coalition (UUUC) emphasized unity of purpose in the conduct of the Convention campaign rather than differences between coalition partners. The Loyalists had good reason to do so, for unity was necessary to win a majority of seats in the Convention. The Loyalists had little doubt that they would take a majority of Protestant votes, but this could be as little as one-third of the total Ulster vote and leave them far short of an overall majority in the Convention. A Convention majority required half the vote, and this, if Catholic support was not available, meant taking three-quarters of the Protestant vote. The Loyalists' desire to have the

Convention come down on their side was symbolized by a poster showing a tricolor and a Union Jack balanced in a pair of scales. The slogan was: "Tip the Scale. Vote UUUC."

The unity of action of the UUUC was demonstrated in a series of difficult decisions about the number of coalition candidates to be nominated in each constituency. In 1973, when the electoral strength of the different parties was unknown, DUP, VUP, and anti-Faulkner Unionist candidates had been so numerous that the Loyalist vote had been divided and Loyalist candidates eliminated in successive STV counts rather than strengthened by votes transferred to each other. While the UUUC wished to nominate fewer candidates, each member of the coalition wished to nominate the maximum number of candidates to strengthen its position within the coalition as well as within the Assembly. A committee consisting of representatives of each of the three Loyalist parties was established to determine how many candidates each party should nominate in each constituency to give the UUUC its best chance of winning the most seats.

The UUUC coalition held together through a winter of hard bargaining for seats. The coalition nominated sixty-two candidates: eighteen DUP, seventeen Vanguard, twenty-six Official Unionist, and one independent Loyalist. By comparison with the 1973 Assembly election, Vanguard dropped from twenty-five to seventeen candidates and the Democratic Unionists went up one to eighteen candidates, while the Unionists, who had had fifty-six candidates in 1973—albeit split between Faulknerites and Loyalists—nominated twenty-seven candidates to fight the Convention election.[8] The total of sixty-two candidates anticipated a maximum of fifty Loyalist seats in the Convention, if one goes by the rule of thumb that a party should nominate one candidate more than it expects to get elected in each constituency so that the elimination of its "extra" candidate will transfer votes to put in another member of the slate.

A total of fifty-three candidates referred to both the UUUC endorsement and to their party label in describing themselves on the ballot paper. Six referred only to the coalition endorsement, including William Craig, leader of the Vanguard Unionists. Craig was the only

---

[8] Tabulations of candidates and votes reported in this study include, in addition to three party categories, a fourth generic category of Loyalist candidates not officially linked with the UUUC parties. One such successful candidate, F. Millar, North Belfast, was an independent with UUUC endorsement, whereas Hugh Smyth, the other elected Loyalist, did not have its endorsement, but rather a UVF background. Loyalists also include McFarland and Elliott, East Belfast, and Trimble, West Belfast. Roy Bradford, an Official Unionist candidate in East Belfast, is counted with the OU group: he neither received nor sought the UUUC endorsement.

member of the Westminster Parliament to refer to his Westminster seat in his ballot paper designation. Gerry Fitt, James Kilfedder and Ian Paisley, the other Westminster M.P.s contesting Convention seats, did not think it worth mentioning their place in the British House of Commons, aptly reflecting Ulster priorities.

Equally important, the UUUC showed the ability to prepare an election manifesto to which all three parties were committed. The manifesto was issued on 16 April in the penthouse nightclub of the Europa Hotel, Belfast, where scantily clad bunny girls normally entertain. Under the headline, "Ulster is an integral part of the United Kingdom," it demanded: [9]

> (1) "Full representation in the Parliament of the United Kingdom" (that is, twenty-one Ulster seats in the British Parliament, the same in proportion to population as Scotland, rather than twelve as at present).
> (2) "A democratically elected Parliament with a system of government broadly in line with the provisions to be made for constitutional devolution in the United Kingdom as a whole."
> a) "We reject as inherently undemocratic any artificial device for giving any political party or interest a larger share of representation, influence or power than that to which its electoral support entitles it."
> b) "The Leader of the party with a majority in the House would be entrusted to form a government."
> c) "The Ulster Parliament and Government should be responsible for policing and internal security."
> (3) Ulster's links with the Crown must be maintained and strengthened.
> (4) "The restoration of democratic local government" (that is, a return of greater powers to elected local authorities and decision-making in committees representing parties in proportion to their strength on the local council).
> (5) "No Council of Ireland" and the explicit rejection of "any imposed institutionalized association with the Irish Republic."
> (6) "Constitutional Rights" (that is, safeguards for the rights of devolved parliaments within the United Kingdom, as well as for the rights of individual citizens).

The UUUC manifesto broadened the customary plea for British constitutional procedures by demanding that Northern Ireland should enjoy the devolved powers that all British parties were currently

---

[9] *United Ulster Unionist Election Manifesto* (Belfast: Century Services, 1975).

promising to Scotland and Wales. It avoided any reference to religion and, in the circumstances of a Protestant vote divided among six pro-British parties, it could not be sure that the majority rule it called for would be tantamount to Protestant rule. It proposed that minority parties be given a voice through backbench committees.

In view of the fissiparous tendencies of Ulster politics, exacerbated as much by personality as by ideology, the UUUC asked each Convention candidate to sign a pledge, witnessed by the chairman of his constituency party as a condition of his receiving coalition endorsement. The pledge read: ". . . I will support the policies of my party and the UUUC and at all times I will obey the coalition and party whips on matters of policy and tactics in the proceedings of the Convention."[10] The pledge was considered necessary by the UUUC as a means of avoiding the divisions that had plagued the Unionist party since the mid-1960s. The vagaries of Ulster politics being what they are, a few candidates of the coalition parties did not sign or were not offered the pledge, and one independent was accepted as a coalition candidate. The incentive for a candidate to pledge support for the manifesto was simple: the coalition urged potential supporters to concentrate their preferences among the three Loyalist parties—and not to vote for candidates of any non-coalition party, which they could technically do with the single transferable vote ballot.

By the eve of the poll, the leaders of the UUUC had made clear that their electoral appeal was focused exclusively upon those who were unyielding in their support of traditional Ulster political values. William Craig, leader of the Vanguard party, praised the actions of the Ulster Workers' Council in helping Ulster people (that is, Protestants) regain "their pride and self-respect."[11] In a campaign speech to the Ulster Workers' Council, he warned the British government, "The Ulster people are a peaceful, democracy-loving race, but we can be pushed too far." Ian Paisley called upon the electorate to repudiate the British-sponsored policies to which he referred in saying that Ulster people "by treachery have seen the Province sold from under them and negotiations under way to betray them."[12] He called for the military defeat rather than "further appeasement" of the IRA. Harry West, leader of the Official Unionists, called for patience and goodwill to work out "a form of government that will be pretty acceptable all round to nearly everybody"—but he also rejected power

---

[10] "Protest at Gag Attempt by UUUC," *Belfast Telegraph*, 24 March 1975.
[11] "Ulster Fears of New Loyalist Strike," *The Times* (London), 21 April 1975.
[12] "Last Words: The Party Leaders Present Their Final Eve-of-Poll Statements," *Belfast Telegraph*, 30 April 1975.

sharing. "In a democracy a majority does have its rights and once the people decide about something fundamental we cannot have a system of government which then reverses their decision." [13]

While the leaders of the UUUC were optimistic about winning three-quarters of the Protestant vote and a majority of the Convention seats, they did not regard the outcome of the election as a certainty. The coalition had won ten out of twelve Westminster seats the previous October, but it had not had to fight each seat against the combined opposition of Brian Faulkner's UPNI, Alliance, and the Northern Ireland Labour party. The introduction of UPNI candidates in every constituency but one created an important unknown factor for the UUUC. In 1973, the Democratic Unionists and Vanguard Unionists together had taken but fifteen of seventy-eight Assembly seats, and allied anti-power-sharing, anti-Faulkner Unionists had won another twelve seats, giving the Loyalists twenty-seven of the seventy-eight seats in the Assembly. Thus, they needed to add thirteen to their strength to secure a majority; these could come from the seats won by the Faulkner Unionists and perhaps from the eight seats won by Alliance in 1973. Party managers expected a small majority—but not an inevitable majority. There was more than pious pleasantry in Ian Paisley's reply to a reporter's question, "If the SDLP, Alliance and Faulkner Unionists can get a majority coalition, we as democrats will accept Opposition in those circumstances." [14]

**Intermediate Positions.** The Unionist party of Northern Ireland is an unusual phenomenon in United Kingdom politics, a "presidential-type" party in an election where no one is running for president. After Brian Faulkner had been ejected from the leadership of the Official Unionists, he needed a party to maintain any significance in parliamentary government, where numbers of supporters elected, rather than the number of votes polled by an individual candidate, is of greatest importance. In a French-style ballot for a president of Northern Ireland, Faulkner could have hoped to run well because he is an established personality—and because the remainder of the Protestant vote would probably have been split by the three leaders of the parties in the UUUC. But such a ballot was not available to him. Nor would a vote for a one-man office have been consistent with the philosophy of power sharing, which presupposes coalition in a cabinet-style executive as well as in an elected assembly.

---

[13] Ibid.

[14] "Poppets Make Way for Red, White and Blue Rosettes," *Irish Times*, 17 April 1975.

The UPNI was fighting the election to establish itself as a power-sharing party for which traditional Unionists might vote. Since Unionists of various stripes constituted at least two-thirds of the electorate, it was seeking votes where many votes are to be found. But it was seeking late in the day. The Alliance party had already been working for five years for the support of moderate Unionists, both Protestant and Catholic, starting in the days when Faulkner himself was opposed to the symbolically reformist policies of Terence O'Neill and James Chichester-Clark at Stormont. Since Brian Faulkner was the prime minister who had introduced internment in August 1971, he could hope for little support from Catholic moderates. Among Protestants, Faulkner started with the advantage of having contacts in the Unionist party throughout the Province. (So too, incidentally, did William Craig, leader of the Vanguard Unionists.) Among the eighteen UPNI candidates, thirteen had sat in the 1973 Assembly, and another had been a Westminster M.P. for the constituency he was contesting. The new party fielded candidates in eleven of the Province's twelve constituencies.

The UPNI manifesto gave guarded support to two of the conditions of the British White Paper: power sharing and acceptance of Westminster's role in Northern Ireland's government. But it explicitly rejected anything like a Council of Ireland, which it described as "counterproductive to the development of friendly co-operation on social and economic matters between the Republic and Northern Ireland." [15] Like the UUUC and Alliance manifestos, the UPNI declaration criticized the Republic of Ireland for its territorial claim to Ulster and for its refusal to extradite to Northern Ireland individuals taking refuge there from the RUC. Its endorsement of power sharing read as follows:

> We are prepared to agree that representatives from either of these minority groups [those who favor a United Ireland or an independent Ulster] play a responsible role in government if they are prepared to work for the benefit of all the people of Northern Ireland.[16]

The UPNI thus sought to equate the pro-independence views of some members of the Vanguard Unionists with the Irish unity aspirations of the SDLP in order to place itself in a middle position; it was willing conditionally to work with either. In comments upon Britain's role in Ulster, the UPNI manifesto recognized the value of having a Northern

---

[15] *Union and Partnership* (Belfast: Unionist Party of Northern Ireland manifesto, 1975), p. 5.
[16] Ibid., p. 4.

Ireland secretary in the British cabinet "so that Ulster interests can properly be represented in the Cabinet," but it also argued that the secretary of state should have no veto on any actions taken by elected Ulster politicians.[17]

Brian Faulkner's most notable contribution to the election campaign was a statement issued nine days before the balloting, in which he warned that the British government had secret plans for the repartition of Northern Ireland, with a forced transfer of Protestants to the east of the Province and Catholics to the west. The latter would join the Republic—and eventually force the dismembered Protestant part of Ulster to join the Republic too. Faulkner argued that the possibility of repartition was real, given that direct rule could not be maintained indefinitely and the British government could not withdraw from an integral part of the United Kingdom because of "the rampage of the gunmen which would follow." It would opt for repartition, on· the grounds that, "If the two communities in Ulster cannot live together, they must be separated." The allegation was not supported by any confirming evidence, nor was it picked up by candidates in other parties. An *Irish Times* reporter laconically described it as a statement "in the classic tradition of scare politics." [18] In his election eve statement, Brian Faulkner reaffirmed the UPNI's commitment to "traditional Unionism" and attacked the UUUC coalition partners as "dictators using the name of Unionist." Faulkner left undefined whether the SDLP met his condition for coalition in power sharing: "firm acceptance of our position in the United Kingdom and support for the forces of law and order." [19]

The Northern Ireland Labour party entered the Convention campaign risking less than the Unionist party of Northern Ireland only because it had less to lose. In 1973, the NILP nominated eighteen candidates in nine constituencies, but it won only one seat—David Bleakley was returned without a quota in East Belfast—and lost thirteen deposits. The creation of the SDLP had effectively destroyed its hopes for a substantial vote from Catholics in Belfast, a group previously prepared, in the absence of a Nationalist or Irish Labour candidate, to vote NILP on economic grounds. The party had increasingly been identified with the Unionist and Protestant majority as the Troubles had worn on. The Ulster Workers' Council strike of May 1974

---

17 Ibid.

18 The comment, and Faulkner's views, can be found in Conor O'Clery's article, "Faulkner Voices Fears about the 'Unthinkable and Unspeakable,' " *Irish Times*, 23 April 1975.

19 "Last Words: The Party Leaders Present Their Final Eve-of-Poll Statements."

was a particularly tense moment for the NILP, for the British Labour government dismissed the strikers as "beyond the pale" of negotiation. The NILP could hardly do this, for the strikers were based in East Belfast, the constituency of their Assembly member. Prominent members of the NILP sought to bring the British government and the Ulster Workers' Council together. Their efforts failed, but inevitably branded the party as sympathetic to hardline Loyalist views.

The title page of the Labour party manifesto in 1975, released prematurely before those of other parties, bore the slogan "Support the Link." It showed the hands of Ulster workmen reaching across and down to grasp outstretched hands from Scotland, England, and Wales. There was no hand reaching toward the Republic of Ireland. The NILP rejected North-South cooperation as "impossible" until the Republic abandoned its territorial claim upon Ulster and showed itself ready to extradite suspected terrorists. To the conventional Unionist arguments for the British link, the NILP added three more: the higher standard of living in Britain, a British guarantee of United Kingdom welfare state standards, and the integration of Northern Ireland in the British economy.

By contrast with its position in 1973, the Northern Ireland Labour party did not endorse power sharing, arguing that "no section of the people should be given the right of veto over the establishment of regional government structures." It advanced as an alternative the remodelling of Stormont to provide for committee management of each area of government formerly headed by a minister. The chairmen of the departmental committees would constitute the Executive or cabinet. Membership of each committee would include representatives of all parties in proportion to their numbers in the assembly, and each party could speak up on issues prior to the decision stage. By the same token the committees would be assured a pro-Union majority, and any party with a majority in the Assembly could name all the committee chairmen if it wished.[20] In an eve-of-poll message, David Bleakley conceded that the committee scheme might not work. As an alternative, he urged what other parties rejected: "a continuation of direct rule from Britain to protect our citizenship, to give effective security and to develop and strengthen the social and economic framework." [21]

The NILP manifesto called for "a genuine peace in our community" and attacked the Provisional IRA. It was silent about the activities of Protestant paramilitary organizations, such as the UDA, which

---

[20] *Support the Link* (Belfast: Northern Ireland Labour Party, 1975).
[21] "Last Words: The Party Leaders Present Their. Final Eve-of-Poll Statements."

has headquarters in East Belfast, but its silence did not last throughout the campaign. Journalists noted that at least two NILP candidates had contacts with Protestant paramilitary organizations. During the campaign, a group of trade unionists, including members of the party's Executive, established a Trade Union and Labour Co-Ordination Group. In the words of its chairman, Paddy Doherty, "The manifesto promotes the Union from beginning to end as if nothing else mattered, sometimes in language more extreme than that used by old-time Unionists. We want to notify people that we disagree, and that there is still a nonsectarian socialist voice in Northern Ireland." [22] With only six candidates contesting seats in four constituencies, the voice of both proponents and critics of the NILP manifesto was bound to be a small one.

The Alliance party entered the Convention election as a party that had always sought votes from both Protestants and Catholics. Theoretically, it was appealing for votes from everyone in Northern Ireland. But in a society where denominational labels are significant, it ran the practical risk of getting no votes, as a party that was neither "one thing nor t'other." The party's showing in 1973 had earned it a place in the power-sharing Executive, though its Assembly leader, Oliver Napier, was not prominent in his role as law reform advisor. Alliance's participation also provided a coalition makeweight against the Faulkner Unionists, for the SDLP and Alliance together had more seats in the Assembly than the Faulkner Unionists.

To symbolize its position as the David between the two Goliaths of the UUUC and the SDLP, the Alliance party launched its manifesto in a modest first-floor meeting room of the Europa Hotel. The manifesto brought together elements found in the manifestos of several different parties. Like the SDLP and the UPNI, Alliance explicitly favored power sharing. Like the UUUC, it favored increased Ulster representation in Westminster on the basis of parity with Scotland and Wales. Like the UUUC and the Republican Clubs, Alliance favored a bill of rights. On the Irish dimension, the manifesto combined SDLP and Unionist sentiments:

> We accept the need for practical co-operation between North and South on many issues which are of common concern to both parts of Ireland. . . . The present constitutional claim by the Republic of sovereignty over Northern Ireland is a formidable barrier against better relations.[23]

---

[22] "Loyalist Links Make Trade Unionists Unhappy with N.I.L.P. Campaign," *Irish Times*, 24 April 1975.

[23] "Convention Must Survey Kinds of Partnership Government," *Irish Times*, 17 April 1975, containing the text of the Alliance party manifesto.

The manifesto was the most explicit of any party's in detailing views on the police and security:

We are convinced that peace, security and prosperity will never come to our Province until the law is rigorously enforced in all areas and until every citizen is afforded its protection. Policies such as internment are counterproductive and serve only to undermine public confidence in law and order. We view with contempt those politicians who have entered into pacts with paramilitary organisations, whether Republican or Loyalist, and who have given tacit support to criminal conspiracies of evil men in the name of patriotism.

The key to the defeat of the murderers and gangsters who prey on our people is effective policing in all areas. Successive British governments have failed to come to grips with this reality. It cannot be said that there is any positive policing policy for Northern Ireland. . . .

We will continue to press for a high-powered Police Authority to control the RUC and for an independent complaints tribunal.[24]

Unintentionally, Alliance produced a slogan—"In your heart you know it's right"—that almost exactly duplicated that of Barry Goldwater in his disastrous campaign for the American presidency in 1964. Of the twenty-three Alliance candidates, eight were Catholics. The usual pattern was to nominate two candidates in a constituency, one Protestant and one Catholic. (One candidate was also an ex-Unionist member at Stormont, and two candidates had brothers contesting Convention seats for the SDLP.) During the campaign, Alliance candidates were ready to attack both SDLP and Loyalist opponents in their search for votes in both communities. In an eve-of-poll message, Oliver Napier emphasized Alliance's forthright condemnation of the men of violence, whether claiming to be Republican or Loyalist. He added pointedly, "It has saddened me to see some other political parties fail to do likewise."[25]

**The Catholic Alternatives.** Two campaigns were conducted concurrently within the Catholic community. The first was about whether to vote, the second about whom to vote for. After considering the idea of running candidates in the first flush of the truce negotiated with the British government, the Provisional Sinn Fein finally decided that it would call upon its supporters to boycott the election. In a state-

---

24 Ibid.

25 "Last Words: The Party Leaders Present Their Final Eve-of-Poll Statements."

ment justifying its boycott decision, it repeated conventional Republican rhetoric: "The six-county state was originally and still is an artificial creation, and the type of discussion proposed is unrealistic until Britain declares her intention of withdrawing from Ireland." A British journalist translated the Provisional Sinn Fein's main reason for deciding not to participate as, "that it would be thrashed at an election." [26] Ruairi O'Bradaigh, the Provisional Sinn Fein leader from Dublin, used a social club in a Catholic ghetto area of West Belfast to launch the "boycott manifesto." By contrast, the breakaway Irish Republican Socialist party like the other parties used the Europa Hotel to launch its boycott manifesto. Its boycott incidentally meant that Bernadette Devlin McAliskey, an IRSP supporter, would not be a candidate for a Convention seat.

In Irish politics, which gave the word to the world, "to boycott" is a verb of action. Provisional Sinn Fein actively campaigned to get people to stay away from the polls on election day. In a parody of press advertisements instructing voters how to mark a PR ballot, Sinn Fein advertised: "How to boycott. It's as Easy as 1, 2, 3. (1) Stay at Home. (2) Forget about Elections. (3) Refuse to be used . . . BOY-COTT." [27] A Provisional Sinn Fein poster attacked power sharing by depicting a prostrate figure stabbed in the back by a dagger with SDLP written on the blade and a Union Jack on the handle.

In the circumstances of a boycott campaign, SDLP organizers welcomed the decision of the Republican Clubs (connected with the Official side) to contest the election, for this effectively split Republicans on the issue of whether or not to vote. Individuals could go to the polls saying that they intended to vote Republican and in the secrecy of the ballot booth cast a vote for the SDLP. The Republican Clubs' manifesto made clear that the group was not altering most of its traditional outlook. It declared that the best way to end "British control and exploitation of Ireland, North and South" was through the "withdrawal of British political and economic control" and the creation of an all-Ireland Irish Socialist Republic, replacing reactionary institutions in Dublin, as well as the old Stormont regime.[28] It claimed that power sharing between Protestants and Catholics was irrelevant. Ireland needed political institutions that gave power to the workers. Republicans said that if elected they would oppose the Convention's commencing work until all internees had been released.

---

[26] See "Mr. Wilson Names May 1 as Date for Ulster Election."

[27] Advertisement in the *Irish News* (Belfast), 1 May 1975.

[28] See "Republicans Blame British Control," *Belfast Telegraph*, 17 April 1975, a story concerning the Republican manifesto.

The Republican Clubs were ready to test their popular support by nominating seventeen candidates, only one less than Brian Faulkner's Unionist party of Northern Ireland. Their candidates stood in eight of twelve constituencies, avoiding only the strongly Protestant constituencies of North Down and North Antrim and East and South Belfast. Their campaign workers suffered harassment from several sides. British security forces were watching a number of party workers including ex-internees in their ranks. Republicans were targets for Protestant assassination groups, and Provisional and IRSP Republicans were bitterly feuding with the Official Republican movement. The Republican Clubs got through the campaign without losing any candidates: only a few shots were fired and no candidates or party workers were jailed. Notwithstanding its nominal appeal to unite working-class people, in an eve-of-poll message, Malachy McGurran, chairman of the Ulster Republican Clubs, stressed the need for a new type of police force to patrol the Catholic community.[29]

The SDLP election manifesto, "Speak with Strength," differed greatly from the UUUC manifesto in that the latter concentrated solely upon constitutional issues, whereas the former offered a general review of the political situation more suitable for a normal general election campaign.[30] The SDLP stressed the achievements of an "experienced team" of politicians who had established themselves in the five years since the party was founded. It also emphasized the importance of economic progress in Ulster. While recognizing "a deep division between our two traditions," it called for a new departure, because the historic principles of each community "have always resulted in conflict, death and destruction, and in a deepening of bitterness and division." It stated as the party's basic principles:

1. A powerful and representative Northern Ireland Assembly.
2. An administration in which both sections of the community participate to the full.
3. The recognition and acceptance of the Irish Dimension.
4. The recognition and acceptance of the British Dimension.

The manifesto asserted that power sharing and an Irish dimension offered the best method for achieving economic as well as political advance. It did not spell out what institutions it envisioned a consti-

---

[29] "Last Words: The Party Leaders Present Their Final Eve-of-Poll Statements."
[30] For quotations, see *Speak with Strength* (Belfast: SDLP Constitutional Convention Election manifesto, 1975).

tutional convention adopting. The institutions most obviously suited to the SDLP specifications were the institutions of the power-sharing Executive that had been repudiated by the Ulster Workers' Council strike twelve months before. Gerry Fitt, the party leader, concluded the manifesto press conference with the cautious comment, "I am not of the opinion that the Convention won't work." [31]

The SDLP first and foremost wished to defend its claim to be the exclusive spokesman for the Catholic community and thus maintain its monopoly claim to a seat in any power-sharing group that might subsequently emerge. To do this it had to prevent Republicans from winning seats—or damaging SDLP chances through an effective boycott campaign. The party had most to fear in the rural constituencies west of the River Bann, where Republicans had run well in Westminster elections. The SDLP differentiated itself from the Republican Clubs, which called for an end to internment before the Convention could commence, by stating that it would negotiate to create a broadly based system of government first, and then give full support and respect to its police service. The SDLP also faced a challenge in West Belfast from Tom Conaty, chairman of the Central Citizens' Defence Committee. Conaty asserted that the SDLP "do not accurately reflect the current thinking and priorities of the Catholic people" and claimed that he was the only properly Catholic candidate.[32]

The SDLP also had positive visions of the stakes that could be won if it continued to hold a monopoly claim to represent the Catholic community. Denis Haughey, the party's chairman, declared flatly, "We will accept nothing less than Cabinet positions in government." While the goal was clear, the means were kept flexible. Ben Caraher, party vice-chairman, emphasized this: "At various times we advocated various institutions. We haven't fixed ourselves to any form of institution and we are not tying ourselves now, but maintaining ourselves on these principles," that is, the four general principles enumerated above.[33] The SDLP hoped that it might win up to three additional seats in the eastern part of the Province by drawing some moderate Protestant as well as Catholic votes. If it could increase its numbers in the Convention, this would strengthen its bargaining position, even though the SDLP would still have far less than a majority of seats.

---

[31] "SDLP Confidence Not Rated in Provisional SF Poll," *Irish Times*, 16 April 1975.

[32] See full-page advertisement, "Conaty—Independent," *Irish News*, 22 April 1975.

[33] For Haughey and Caraher's views, see "SDLP Confidence Not Rated in Provisional SF Poll."

As a new party, the SDLP claimed that it was not responsible for the failings of the Nationalists in the past. It called upon Loyalists to repudiate historic Unionist principles that, in the words of Gerry Fitt, the SDLP leader, "led to the unspeakable horror and brutal carnage that has afflicted this society over the past six years." [34] In a final television appeal for the vote, John Hume, a senior SDLP figure, described the Province's political circumstances thus:

> We must find a new way forward and we can only do so by facing reality, the reality that we have differences here, fundamental differences. We accept the difference, the only way forward is not conflict, it is partnership between both our traditions. . . .
> Partnership is the means whereby both sections of this community in both parts of this island can develop understanding and trust and confidence to replace the bigotry, the fear, the violence in the past. At the end of the road, we do not know what will be there, but it is bound to be good, because it will be something that will have evolved, that will have been agreed between the people of this island, and this is surely something that we can all strive for. [35]

Hume added, "We have no illusions about the difficulty in achieving that, but we must begin somewhere."

## On the Eve of the Election

By the time the nominations had closed, one thing was clear: no one party would win a majority of seats in the Convention, for no party had nominated sufficient candidates to win forty seats. The SDLP fielded the largest number of candidates, thirty, the Official Unionists twenty-seven, the Democratic Unionists and the Unionist party of Northern Ireland eighteen each, Vanguard and the Republican Clubs seventeen each, and the Northern Ireland Labour party six. Agreement in the Convention could only come from a coalition of parties. Up to a point, coalition involves consensus, inasmuch as different parties must agree to bury differences for the sake of unity. But the unity of coalition need not be the consensus which the British government has vainly sought for years. It could be the consensus of a majority held together by the reward of gaining all the power that comes to a coalition with one more than half the seats in an assembly ruled by majority vote.

---

[34] "Last Words: The Party Leaders Present Their Final Eve-of-Poll Statements."
[35] Quoted from a typed transcript of a BBC T.V. broadcast of 29 April 1975, kindly made available by BBC-Northern Ireland.

Only one group of parties—the Loyalists—fought the election as a coalition. Notwithstanding significant differences concerning alliances with paramilitary groups, personalities, internment, and the attractions of Ulster independence, the three UUUC parties pledged to work together to achieve an agreed set of constitutional aims. The opponents of the Loyalists were not similarly united. The three former partners in the power-sharing Executive, the Faulkner-led UPNI, the Alliance, and the SDLP, competed with each other for votes. Up to a point, there was no competition, for the SDLP could realistically only expect to draw first-preference votes from Catholics and the Unionist party of Northern Ireland from Protestants. But there was potential value in asking supporters to transfer lower-preference votes to the other power-sharing parties. There was incentive to make such an electoral pact, especially for the weaker Alliance and UPNI group, because in a number of constituencies, each party might expect to win at least half a quota of votes. A pact offered the prospect of the partners winning two or even three seats by pooling votes, rather than one or none. But such a pact was not practical in ideological terms, for the commitments of the three parties on basic issues were often at variance. For example, only the SDLP upheld an Irish dimension, and the UPNI under Brian Faulkner could not be disassociated from a hard-line policy on internment. Another reason for hesitancy was that none of the power-sharing parties was confident that such an agreement would win it more votes than it might lose if it aligned itself publicly with partners whose views were, in some ways, in conflict with those of the party's core of supporters.

Ironically, the one point about which every party but the weak NILP agreed was that Northern Ireland should be governed, as the SDLP manifesto put it, by "a powerful and representative Northern Ireland Assembly." The agreement was negative, as the various manifestos made clear. It provided little comfort, however, to the silent partner in the election campaign, the British government, for the White Paper authorizing the Convention election had stated that, while the purpose of the Convention was to propose a constitution, the power to dispose of the government of Northern Ireland remained, in formal legal terms at least, with the British government at Westminster. To what extent Britain could hope to realize its power depended not only upon the invisible bonds of an unwritten constitution, but also upon the preferences Ulstermen displayed in the election.

# 5
# THE RESULT OF THE BALLOT

*It is the same old faces with the some old arguments.*
*It never worked before so why should it work now?*

Ulster housewife to reporter

Only one party leader, Gerry Fitt of the SDLP, noted any symbolism in the date set for the Convention election, 1 May, the internationally celebrated day of trade union and working class solidarity. And no party leader publicized that the date was symbolic in another sense as well: May Day in Morse code is an internationally recognized symbol of distress. In the final week of the campaign, six Ulstermen were killed in four separate shooting and bombing incidents; the dead included the leader of the Official IRA in Belfast, Billy McMillan, shot in what appeared to be an episode of the IRA/IRSP factional feud. The day before polling, a spokesman for the paramilitary Protestant Action Group claimed that its members had murdered seven Roman Catholics in the previous two weeks. Polling day was relatively uneventful: no one was killed, but the homes or automobiles of two candidates were bombed, Republican Club election workers were shot at in the Lower Falls area of Belfast, and policemen taking away ballot boxes to the count were stoned by hundreds of demonstrators in the Creggan area of Londonderry.

## Turnout and Boycott

The overall turnout for the Convention election was 65.8 percent, a decline of 6.5 percentage points from the turnout at the 1973 Assembly election, and of 1.9 percentage points from the October

95

1974 Westminster ballot in the Province. This was the third lowest turnout for any of the fourteen elections for Ulster representative assemblies that have taken place in the last half-century. The low turnout occurred in spite of the fact that the qualification for postal voting is more liberal than in Great Britain. This was intended to encourage people to vote at home, if they feared intimidation or violence at polling stations.[1] In the Convention election, 8.0 percent of the total electorate voted by post, including 20.8 percent of the voters in Mid-Ulster and 20.2 percent of the voters in Fermanagh and South Tyrone, both rural constituencies where the Republicans are relatively strong; nearly one in every eight ballots counted was a postal ballot.

The hope of Provisional Sinn Fein to secure a massive boycott of the Convention election was not realized. Some nonvoting is inevitable, because the electoral register is compiled only once a year, in the autumn; it necessarily includes the names of people who have died or left the troubled Province by the time of a May election. When turnout approaches 100 percent of the registered electorate, the likelihood rises that impersonation or fraud has occurred. An indicator of the effect of the Provisional boycott is, ironically, the tabulation of spoiled ballots. This traditional Sinn Fein tactic prevents anyone else from impersonating the voter, as well as providing an official tally of protest votes. In 1973, spoiled ballots were cast by 1.6 percent of the total electorate; in 1975, the total was 2.7 percent. The largest proportion of spoiled votes was in Fermanagh and South Tyrone, 3.0 percent, which also had the highest turnout of any constituency, 78.4 percent. Overall, there was a very high correlation between the proportion of Catholics in a constituency and the number of spoiled ballots. If spoiled ballot papers were overwhelmingly protest votes by Republicans, and if an equal number of Catholics abstained completely from marking ballot papers, then about 3 percent of the electorate supported the Republicans in ways that do not show up in the subsequent tabulation of valid votes cast for political parties.

Because of the importance of the issues and the relative clarity of the parties' positions, the choice offered the Northern Ireland electorate in the Convention election was the most clear-cut since the Stormont ballot of 1965. The answer given by the voters was also clear-cut: a majority voted for candidates of the Loyalist United

---

[1] Postal voting also makes intimidation or corruption easier. In the words of Conor O'Clery, in "Dossier for Secretary of State Cites 'Postal Vote Factory' at Work," *Irish Times*, 21 April 1975, the liberal provision of postal ballots meant: "The Ulster dead have become more sophisticated. They can mark the ballot papers in the privacy of their own graves."

## Table 3
### NORTHERN IRELAND CONVENTION ELECTION RESULT, 1975

| Parties | Votes Number | Votes Percent | Number of Candidates | Number of Seats Won |
|---|---|---|---|---|
| Loyalists | | | | |
| Official Unionists | 169,797 | 25.8 | 27 | 19 |
| DUP (Paisleyites) | 97,073 | 14.7 | 18 | 12 |
| Vanguard | 83,507 | 12.7 | 17 | 14 |
| Other Loyalists | 10,140 | 1.5 | 5 | 2 |
| Total Loyalist | 360,517 | 54.8 | 67 | 47 |
| Alliance party | 64,657 | 9.8 | 23 | 8 |
| Unionist party of Northern Ireland | 50,891 | 7.7 | 18 | 5 |
| NILP | 9,102 | 1.4 | 6 | 1 |
| SDLP | 156,049 | 23.7 | 30 | 17 |
| Republican Clubs | 14,515 | 2.2 | 17 | 0 |
| Independent/others | 2,430 | 0.4 | 4 | 0 |
| TOTAL | 658,161 | 100.0 | 165 | 78 |

**Note:** The size of the total electorate was 1,026,987. The total number of votes was 676,151 (65.8 percent) including 17,990 (2.7 percent) spoiled ballots.

**Source:** Derived from McAllister, *The 1975 Northern Ireland Convention Election.*

Ulster Unionist Council. With 54.8 percent of the votes cast and forty-seven of the seventy-eight seats, the Loyalists won greater popular support than any party has registered in a general election in Britain in more than forty years. The Loyalist Coalition won more than twice the votes and more than twice the seats of their chief competitor, the Social Democratic and Labour party. Brian Faulkner's Unionist party of Northern Ireland, which sought to constitute a bridge between traditional Unionists and the power-sharing coalition desired by the SDLP, was trounced; it won only 7.7 percent of the vote and five seats.[2]

---

[2] For the most detailed presentation of convention election results, from which the tables herein have been derived, see Ian McAllister, *The 1975 Northern Ireland Convention Election* (Glasgow: University of Strathclyde Survey Research Centre, Occasional Paper No. 14, 1975).

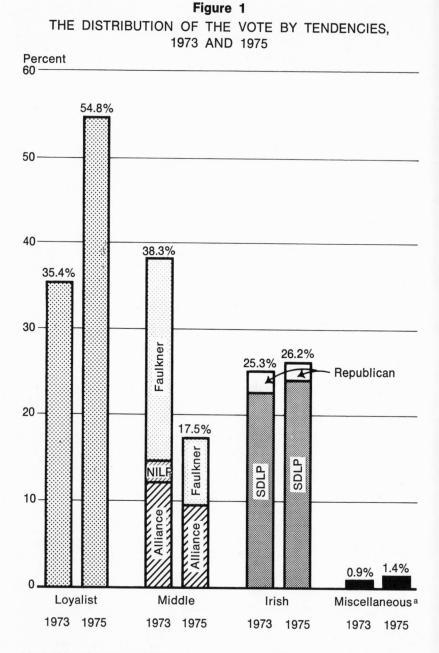

**Figure 1**

THE DISTRIBUTION OF THE VOTE BY TENDENCIES, 1973 AND 1975

Percent

a Including the NILP in 1975.

**Source:** Derived from Ian McAllister, *The 1975 Northern Ireland Convention Election* (Glasgow: University of Strathclyde Survey Research Center, Occasional Paper 14, 1975).

## The Distribution of Votes

The overall pattern of the vote in 1973 and 1975 can easily be represented in a diagram showing the proportion of the total vote won by each of the three main groupings: the Loyalists, the parties favoring the Irish dimension (the SDLP and Republicans/Nationalists), and the pro-British pro-power-sharing parties (Alliance and the UPNI). (See Figure 1.) As can be seen, the Loyalists towered over each of the other two groups. The vote for the "middle" parties, on which successive British governments have pinned their hopes, fell to one-sixth of the total from 1973 to 1975. The Irish vote, dominated by support for the SDLP, is significant in a vote about constitutional measures—but not by the standards of a British or American two-party election.

A comparison of the Convention result with the 1973 Assembly election shows that the main political change has resulted from a clarification of the position of the Unionists led by Brian Faulkner.[3] (See Tables 2 and 3.) In 1973, Faulkner led the Official Unionists—albeit a party split by his leadership. In 1973, by blurring his position on power sharing under British terms and by leading the historic governing party of Ulster, Faulkner was able to maximize his electoral support. In 1975, by being identified unambiguously with power sharing under British auspices, Faulkner lost the support of some he had led or misled in 1973. The apparent shift in the popular vote from 1973 does not reflect any substantial change in public opinion. Instead, it reflects a clearer awareness of what the parties stand for and thus how an individual with constant opinions should mark his ballot.

A comparison of the 1975 Convention ballot with the last election for the Stormont Parliament in 1969 underlines the trends revealed from 1973 to 1975. The vote for Irish candidates (in 1969, civil rights and Nationalists) has scarcely altered; it was 23.3 percent in 1969 and 2.6 percentage points higher six years later. The chief change has occurred among Protestants. In 1969, Terence O'Neill, who had led a united party in the 1965 election, was challenged by anti-O'Neill Unionists. Pro-O'Neill candidates took 44.9 percent of

---

[3] For an account of voting in 1973, see R. J. Lawrence, S. Elliott and M. J. Laver, *The Northern Ireland General Elections of 1973* (London: Her Majesty's Stationery Office, Cmnd. 5851). For a discussion of Faulkner's strategic dilemma and how he tried to resolve it, see M. J. Laver, *The Theory and Practice of Party Competition: Ulster 1973-75* (Beverly Hills and London: Sage Professional Paper in Contemporary Political Sociology 06-014, 1976).

the vote in 1969, compared to 26.5 percent for Faulkner Unionists in 1973 and 7.7 percent in 1975. The increasingly organized and active Loyalists have seen their vote rise from 22.4 percent for anti-O'Neill candidates in 1969 to 35.4 percent in 1973, then to an absolute majority in the 1975 Convention election. The middle-of-the-road parties of 1969, Northern Ireland Labour and the Liberals, polled 9.4 percent of the vote then. The heir to their position, the Alliance party, took 9.8 percent of the vote in 1973, and almost the same again in 1975.

Within the Loyalist Coalition, the Official Unionists polled the most votes—25.8 percent of the total—and also took the most seats—nineteen. By fighting as a united party for the first time in a decade, the anti-power-sharing Unionists doubled their vote of 1973 and increased their seats by eight. But the Official Unionists' vote was halved by comparison with the party's strength in 1965, when it did not have to compete with two other parties for the claim to being the Loyalist standard-bearer.

Together, the Democratic Unionists and the Vanguard Unionists saw their vote increase by 6.1 percentage points, and their representation go up from fifteen to twenty-six seats. The parties' combined share of the Northern Ireland vote exceeded that of the Official Unionists by 1.6 percentage points and their total number of Convention members is seven greater than that of the Official Unionists. The total of the Loyalists was further augmented by the return of two independent Loyalists, Hugh Smyth, West Belfast, a founder of the Volunteer Political party, the electoral wing of the UVF, and Frank Millar, an active Orangeman from North Belfast.

The decline in popular approval for Brian Faulkner's brand of Unionism meant that the majority of assemblymen standing for re-election as UPNI candidates were defeated and Faulkner himself finished a humiliating seventh behind three UUUC candidates and three SDLP candidates in the contest for first preference votes in South Down, an area he had represented at Stormont since 1949.

The Alliance party held its own against competition from both the UPNI and SDLP, winning eight seats in 1975 as in 1973. Alliance lost a seat that it had won in 1973 in North Belfast, but gained a seat in South Belfast. As in 1973, Alliance candidates polled far better in constituencies around Belfast than in more traditional rural Ulster.

The Northern Ireland Labour party saw its position little altered by its aggressive support for the link with Britain. Its vote fell to the lowest total in its history, and only one candidate, David Bleakley (East Belfast), was elected, albeit without reaching a quota.

The Social Democratic and Labour party saw its share of the vote rise by 1.6 percentage points, but its representation at Stormont dropped by two seats because, by small margins, it lost seats it had previously held in Armagh and in Mid-Ulster. SDLP candidates there complained of intimidation by armed Republicans preventing Catholics from reaching the polling stations, and also of the theft of postal ballots from supporters. (In fact, the fall in turnout in Armagh was the least in the Province; in Mid-Ulster, it was second highest, behind North Antrim.) In the more peaceful parts of the Province, the SDLP failed to win a third seat in West Belfast, as would have occurred if the party had polled the same strength it registered in the October 1974 Westminster election. The SDLP's attempt to win votes by nominating candidates thought to appeal to liberal Protestants as well as Catholics failed to gain it any additional seats in competition with Alliance candidates.

The candidates of the Republican Clubs fared badly throughout the Province, failing to win any seats. The best Republican results were in Mid-Ulster, where three candidates together took 6.4 percent of first-preference votes, in Armagh, where they took 6.3 percent of first-preference votes, and in West Belfast, where they won 3.7 percent. Tom Conaty, standing as a Catholic independent, also took 5.7 percent of first-preference votes in West Belfast. Had the Republican vote in the Convention election equalled that for Republican sympathizers and candidates at the 1974 Westminster elections, the Republicans would have taken one or more seats in the constituency of Fermanagh and South Tyrone, and at least one seat in Mid-Ulster.

The relative weakness of parties is indicated by the number of deposits (£150, approximately $300) their candidates forfeited. In the STV proportional representation system, a candidate forfeits a deposit if he fails to obtain during the count one-quarter of the quota needed for election. Republican Club candidates were weakest; fifteen of their seventeen candidates forfeited their deposits, a worse showing than in 1973. Half of the six NILP candidates forfeited their deposits. Among other parties, greater care in nominating candidates reduced the number of lost deposits by comparison with 1973. Four of the eighteen UPNI candidates lost deposits and five of the twenty-three Alliance candidates. Only two of the thirty SDLP candidates lost deposits, and none of the UUUC candidates failed to poll enough votes to save his face and his £150.

## The Effects of Proportional Representation

Given the frequency of charges of gerrymandering in Northern Ireland elections, it is particularly important to examine the extent to which the election result allotted seats in proportion to votes. English critics of voting under the old Stormont system often fixed upon features of the system *as it applied to local government:* the way in which ward boundaries and archaic franchise laws enabled Protestant minorities to win a majority of seats in a small number of towns in the Province.[4] They ignored the fact that any fairly drawn boundaries would give Protestants the right to elect approximately two-thirds of any Northern Ireland assembly as long as they continued to constitute two-thirds of the population of the Province. Moreover, they also ignored the distorting effect of the "winner-take-all" electoral system used to elect British M.P.s and members of the old Stormont Parliament. Under that system, the party whose candidate finishes second in a constituency gets nothing for its votes, whether they amount to 1 percent or 49 percent of the total. Inevitably, Catholic candidates were more likely to finish second in Northern Ireland and therefore to suffer from an electoral system that English and American writers regard as normal and desirable.

The change to proportional representation in Northern Ireland provides a test of whether Protestant representation at Stormont was a function of the machinations of Ulster politicians or of the mechanics of an electoral system commonly endorsed by Anglo-American politicians. The logic of electoral systems implies the following hypothesis: the Northern Ireland election system today is *fairer* than the electoral system used to return a British Parliament, insofar as fairness is assessed by the extent to which seats are allotted in proportion to votes.

Within the course of one year, Northern Ireland voters twice cast ballots for representatives. In October 1974, they voted in a "first-past-the-post" election for twelve members of the Westminster Parliament. The result showed a substantial departure from the criterion of fairness defined above: The Loyalists, with 58.4 percent of the vote, took 83.3 percent of the seats (a difference of + 24.9 percentage points), whereas the SDLP, with 22.0 percent of the vote, took but 8.3 percent of the seats (a difference of − 13.7 percentage points). Alliance and UPNI candidates together took 11.8 percent of the vote

---

[4] For an assessment of the likely limits of gerrymandering, see The Cameron Commission, *Disturbances in Northern Ireland*, p. 56 ff.

and received no seats (−11.8 percentage points). Only the Republican candidates were fortuitously treated equitably by the British parliamentary electoral system, taking 8.3 percent of the representation with 7.7 percent of the vote (+0.6 percentage point difference).

In the May 1975 Convention election, the preferences of the Ulster electorate were much the same as they had been in the previous autumn's Westminster contest. The fluctuations in the share of the vote taken by different political groups arises primarily from the fact that under the winner-take-all ballot, most parties did not find it worthwhile to enter a candidate in every constituency, as they do under proportional representation. In the Convention election, there were no substantial discrepancies between the votes a party won and the seats it gained in the Convention. The Loyalists once again gained slightly more seats than their share of the vote entitled them to, but the excess was 5.5 percentage points, as against 24.9 percentage points in the Westminster election. Similarly, the SDLP once again fared worse in seats than in votes, but the difference under PR was 1.9 percentage points, as against 13.7 percentage points under the British-type electoral system.

The greater fairness of the Northern Ireland Convention election can also be demonstrated by comparing the relationship between votes and seats with the outcome of the October 1974 British general election for all 635 seats in the Westminster Parliament. Table 4 confirms that it is the British rather than the Northern Ireland system that today departs most from the principle of "one man, one vote, one value." In 1974, both the Labour and Conservative parties received far more seats than their shares of the vote entitled them to, whether judged in absolute terms or by comparison with Northern Ireland parties in the Convention election. Equally, the Liberals were given a smaller share of seats by the British system than Catholic parties had ever been reduced to at Stormont, whether under proportional representation or a first-past-the-post electoral system. A comparison of the outcome of the Northern Ireland elections with STV proportional representation elections in the Republic of Ireland shows that the Ulster Convention ballot is freer from charges of bias or of intentional gerrymandering than electioneering in its neighbor state.[5]

In one sense the smallest parties gained most from the workings of the proportional representation system, because six of their fourteen successful candidates were elected without reaching the quota.

---

[5] See John H. Whyte, "Ireland: Politics without Social Bases," in Richard Rose, ed., *Electoral Behavior: A Comparative Handbook* (New York: Free Press, 1974), pp. 626–28.

## Table 4
## RELATION OF SEATS TO VOTES, NORTHERN IRELAND AND THE UNITED KINGDOM
### (in percent)

| | Ulster: Convention Election 1975 | | | United Kingdom: Parliamentary Election, October 1974 | | | |
|---|---|---|---|---|---|---|---|
| Party | Votes | Seats | Difference | Party | Votes | Seats | Difference |
| Loyalists | 54.8 | 60.3 | +5.5 | Labour | 39.3 | 50.2 | +10.9 |
| SDLP | 23.7 | 21.8 | −1.9 | Conservative | 35.8 | 43.6 | +7.8 |
| Alliance | 9.8 | 10.2 | +0.4 | Liberal | 18.3 | 2.0 | −16.3 |
| UPNI | 7.7 | 6.4 | −0.7 | Scot-Welsh Nationalist | 3.4 | 2.2 | −1.2 |
| NILP | 1.4 | 1.3 | −0.1 | Ulster parties | 2.4 | 1.9 | −0.5 |
| Others and independents | 2.7 | 0 | −2.7 | Others | 0.8 | 0 | 0.8 |

Source: Calculated from official returns.

This was apt to happen because Alliance, UPNI, and Northern Ireland Labour party candidates could not count on substantial transfers of votes from traditional Protestant or Catholic voters. If one of their candidates did reasonably well in first preferences but failed to secure a quota at an early count, he was unlikely to gain many additional votes, once his running mates had been eliminated. Such a candidate could win only if the Loyalist and SDLP candidates consumed their transferred votes in taking the first several seats and had no surplus left to transfer as the counts progressed, forcing vacancies to be filled by candidates without quotas. The Loyalists took fourteen of their forty-seven seats without quotas, a tribute to their skill in placing sufficient candidates around the Province to poll a maximum, without so dividing the vote among individuals that candidates would be eliminated as the counts progressed. Only three of the seventeen SDLP winners were elected without quotas.

Another test of the equity of an electoral system is the proportion of the votes that are wasted, that is, cast for candidates who remain runners-up after the last seat is filled by a transfer of votes. (Votes cast for candidates with few first-preference votes are not wasted, because they are transferred in early counts and help those who receive them achieve the required quota.) In the 1973 Assembly election, 67,860 votes were thus wasted, 9.4 percent of the total first-preference votes cast. In 1975, 68,686 votes were wasted, 10.4 percent of the total. In both elections, the biggest parties wasted the most votes because they polled the most votes. The amount of waste was minimal: one candidate is necessarily a runner-up in each constituency, as the price of determining the final seat. In both years, the proportion of wasted votes was far less than it is in a Westminster parliamentary election, where more than 10 million votes are always cast for the losing side. In October 1974, for example, 380 of the 635 Westminster seats were won by candidates who polled less than half the vote, and a majority of British constituents "wasted" their ballots.

## The Discipline of Voters

The requirement that each voter cast his vote by numbering his preferences among candidates within a constituency provides important information about the extent to which a political party represents a cohesive group of voters who prefer it above all other parties, or the extent to which voters are attracted by the personalities of individual candidates. Because the ballot allows an individual to list as many (or as few) preferences as he likes, he can also indicate whether the party that receives his first vote is his unique preference or whether there are other parties that he would support once his favorite candidate was out of the running. Another way to make the same point is to note that a voter who refuses to extend his preferences to a second or third choice party is actually indicating that there are some parties he would never vote for. At a certain point, he leaves his ballot blank, refusing to cross an invisible but important line that separates his side from the other side in Ulster politics.

The single transferable vote electoral system, which in Northern Ireland entails an aggregate of more than 100 counts, provides far more information about the political loyalties of voters than does the simple ballot of a British general election. First of all, the results of the Convention election can be analyzed to measure the strength of partisanship. The theory of the STV ballot is that partisanship is weak or nonexistent. Electors vote for individual candidates one at a time, and the rules assume (as the British government had assumed) that individuals will continue to vote for the candidates of other parties as and when their own party's candidates are no longer in the running. In other words, the Northern Ireland elections allow voters to split their tickets, as American voters can. In a normal British parliamentary contest or under the system used in elections to the old Stormont Parliament, an elector cannot split his ticket, for he can only cast a single vote for a single candidate for one constituency.

The first question an elected politician is likely to ask is: where does my vote come from? In the STV ballot, it can come not only from those who put his party first, but also from those who see it as a second best or a lesser evil than other parties. The question is important, not only in considering election results, but also in considering the dynamics of coalition in an assembly or convention. A party that draws a significant proportion of its vote from outside its ranks will be peculiarly sensitive to the wishes of its least firm supporters. What is true of the party in aggregate is even more true of individuals, who will not want to lose seats that they have won through vote transfers by doing anything to alienate voters who supported them as a second choice.

Only the Loyalists and the SDLP drew more than half their total transfer vote from within their own ranks. (See Table A-1.) This reflects, in the first place, the strength of each of these parties: they have several candidates who can stay in the running through many counts and who therefore benefit by support transferred from partisan running mates. This is not the case with UPNI, Alliance, or

NILP candidates, who usually go out in early counts and may not have partisan colleagues to whom they can transfer votes. Alliance and the UPNI drew more than half their transfer vote from other parties. Alliance took more than one-quarter of its transfers from the SDLP and one-sixth from the UPNI, reflecting its aspiration to draw both Protestant and Catholic votes. By contrast, the Unionist party of Northern Ireland took nearly all its vote from other pro-British parties. Of its total transfer vote, only 1 percent came from the SDLP. The Northern Ireland Labour party was distinctive in that it drew more transfers from the Loyalist Coalition than from its own partisans, a reflection of the small size of Labour's vote and the large size of the Loyalist vote.

The complementary question is: where does the vote go? To what extent do voters stay within the ranks of their own party, make their ballots nontransferable by leaving lower preferences blank, or, alternatively, transfer to the ranks of another party? A party is sensitive to a "leakage" of votes, whether it results from a weak sense of party identification or from the elimination of a party's candidates which prevents the voter from pursuing his first preference any further.

The Loyalists and the SDLP are the only parties who retain more than half their vote within their ranks when transfers occur. (See Table A-2.) Loyalist voters distributed 87.1 percent of their transfers to fellow Loyalists, and SDLP voters 59.2 percent of their vote to the party's remaining candidates. Only 6 percent of Loyalist candidates effectively gave lower preferences to UPNI candidates supporting their former leader, Brian Faulkner. Even fewer votes were distributed among the other parties in the Convention contest. By contrast, SDLP voters showed a greater readiness to give votes elsewhere, for one-quarter of SDLP transfers went to Alliance candidates. In South Belfast, 87 percent of SDLP votes transferred to Alliance, where a Catholic Alliance candidate was in the running when the one SDLP candidate was eliminated. In North Down, 81.3 percent of the SDLP vote transferred to Alliance, in circumstances similar except that the Alliance candidate was a Protestant. Equally noteworthy is the fact that in subsequent counts in South Belfast and South Antrim, Alliance votes (including a chunk of SDLP transfers) swung to UPNI, indicating a readiness of some SDLP supporters in these constituencies to make Brian Faulkner's party their third choice.

The Alliance party showed a greater ability to keep votes within its ranks than did the UPNI. Nearly two-thirds of UPNI transfers went to Loyalist candidates. Moreover, more Alliance voters pre-

## Table 5
### THE STRENGTH OF PARTISANSHIP

| | Part A: Discipline | | | | Part B: Exclusiveness | | | |
| | Number of transfers[a] | Votes available for transfer | Transferred within party | | Number of eliminations[b] | Votes available for transfer | Nontransferable | |
| Party | | | Number | Percent | | | Number | Percent |
|---|---|---|---|---|---|---|---|---|
| Loyalists | 44 | 121,065 | 110,017 | 90.9 | Nil | — | — | — |
| UPNI | 7 | 11,893 | 8,063 | 67.8 | 5 | 15,120 | 2,198 | 14.5 |
| Alliance | 9 | 16,766 | 12,711 | 75.8 | 8 | 16,415 | 4,849 | 29.5 |
| NILP | 1 | 532 | 357 | 67.1 | 2 | 4,167 | 590 | 14.2 |
| SDLP | 13 | 22,454 | 18,231 | 81.2 | 5 | 10,943 | 2,418 | 22.1 |
| Republican Clubs | 5 | 4,485 | 3,517 | 78.4 | 4 | 10,387 | 5,905 | 56.8 |

[a] Counts when at least one other candidate of the same party was still in the running.
[b] Counts when no other candidate of the same party remained in the running.
**Source:** Calculated from official returns.

ferred to leave their ballots blank rather than transfer preferences to other parties. Among Alliance votes, about one-sixth went to SDLP and UPNI candidates each. The fact that NILP voters were about as ready to transfer to Loyalist as to Alliance candidates illustrates the division of the party into Protestant and moderate groups.

The extent to which voters are strongly disciplined in their partisanship can be measured by calculating the proportion who transfer votes to other candidates of the same party when a colleague is still in the running. For example, after the first count in West Belfast, 95.7 percent of the supporters of John Laird (an Official Unionist) were disciplined, transferring their votes to other Loyalists, and 73.8 percent of Devlin's supporters were disciplined, transferring their preferences to other SDLP candidates. Table 5, part A, shows that discipline is strongest among Loyalists and the SDLP: 90.9 percent of Loyalists transferred their votes to others running with them and 81.2 percent of SDLP voters did likewise. Discipline was high even in the weakest parties, for 67.8 percent of UPNI voters transferred their support within that party's ranks, as did two-thirds of NILP voters in the one constituency where a transfer could occur between fellow partisans.

At some point in an STV ballot, a strongly partisan voter will be offered the opportunity to declare himself an exclusive partisan by refusing to list preferences for candidates of other parties. The figures on vote transfers allow one to calculate the proportion of a party's supporters that do not transfer votes to another party when the last candidate on the party's slate is eliminated. In West Belfast, for example, only 7.5 percent of the vote of a Catholic independent, Tom Conaty, was exclusive to him. Overall, the supporters of the Republican Clubs showed themselves the most exclusive partisans, for more than half preferred to leave their lower preferences blank rather than vote for candidates of other parties (see Table 5, part B). None of the other parties could claim the exclusive loyalty of more than one-third of their voters, according to data on nontransferable votes. No calculations appear for the Loyalists because their slate of candidates was not eliminated in any of the twelve constituencies. Only one in seven of the supporters of the Unionist party of Northern Ireland or of the NILP showed an exclusive loyalty to his own party. The great bulk preferred to transfer votes to other parties rather than avoid choosing among lesser-evil parties.

The results of the four elections held in Northern Ireland in less than twenty-four months emphasize the relative stability of Ulster voters—especially by comparison with the parties and the electoral system. At each ballot (see Table 6), the proportion voting for Irish

## Table 6

### VOTES BY TENDENCIES, WESTMINSTER AND NORTHERN IRELAND ELECTIONS, 1973–1975

| Election | Loyalists | | Center[a] | | Irish Unity[b] | |
|---|---|---|---|---|---|---|
| | Percentage of vote | Seats | Percentage of vote | Seats | Percentage of vote | Seats |
| 1973, Northern Ireland Assembly | 35.4 | 27 | 38.3 | 32 | 25.3 | 19 |
| 1974 (February), U.K. Parliament | 51.1 | 11 | 18.7 | 0 | 30.2 | 1 |
| 1974 (October), U.K. Parliament | 58.4 | 10 | 11.8 | 0 | 29.7 | 2 |
| 1975, Northern Ireland Convention | 54.8 | 47 | 17.5 | 13 | 26.2 | 17 |

a Includes various Faulkner Unionists, Alliance, and, except for the 1975 Convention election, NILP candidates.
b SDLP plus various Republican and Nationalist candidates.
**Source:** Derived from McAllister, *The 1975 Northern Ireland Convention Election*, Table V.1.

unity has been between 25 and 30 percent; the maximum indicates support from about nine out of ten Catholics. Ironically, the Irish unity vote has been higher at elections for the Westminster Parliament than in Northern Ireland ballots, because the Republicans make more vigorous efforts to contest seats in the British Parliament. The Loyalist vote has been between 51 and 58 percent at three of the four elections. It was less than that in 1973, only because Brian Faulkner's ambiguous position at that time led some voters to include his candidates within the Loyalist ranks. When center candidates have contested seats on an unambiguous power-sharing platform, their vote has ranged from about 12 to 19 percent. In all three groups, constituency-by-constituency examination of fluctuation in the vote shows that the relatively small movements registered have more often been due to changes in strategies for contesting seats than to substantive changes in electoral opinion. Given the extent to which the British have long prided themselves on the relative stability of the British party system, it is ironic that Northern Ireland elections demonstrate greater stability than Westminster elections in the 1970s— and that this very stability is itself grounds for criticism from London!

## The Winning Candidates

Analyzing the characteristics of candidates elected to the Convention provides another means of comparing the parties. The simplest and inevitably the most significant tabulation is that of the religion of the candidates elected on each party's slate. (See Table 7.) Among the seven parties electing members to the Convention, five were 100 percent Protestant and nominated only Protestant candidates: these were the three parties to the UUUC coalition, the Unionist party of Northern Ireland, and the Northern Ireland Labour party. The power-sharing character of the Unionist party of Northern Ireland meant only that half of its sixteen male candidates were Orangemen and half not. The Alliance party succeeded in electing candidates from both communities and saw six Catholic and nine Protestant candidates go down to defeat. The two Protestants among the SDLP's thirty candidates were both successful, thus providing evidence in support of the party's claim to being a nonsectarian Irish, rather than simply a Catholic Irish, party. The vote for the two SDLP Protestants, Ivan Cooper and John Turnly, however, appears to have come substantially from Catholics. The voters returned three clergymen, the Rev. Ian Paisley and the Rev. William Beattie of the Democratic Unionist party and the Rev. Martin Smyth, Imperial Grand Master of the Orange Order, of the Official Unionists. Mrs. Ian Paisley was also elected to a seat from East Belfast. Two SDLP members, John Hume and Frank Feeley, had at one time studied for the Catholic priesthood.

In their social characteristics, the Convention members are fairly typical of the membership of any representative assembly anywhere

### Table 7
### RELIGIOUS AFFILIATION OF CONVENTION MEMBERS

| Party | Protestant | | Catholic | | Total Number of Members |
|---|---|---|---|---|---|
| | Number | Percent | Number | Percent | |
| Loyalists | 47 | 100 | 0 | 0 | 47 |
| UPNI | 5 | 100 | 0 | 0 | 5 |
| NILP | 1 | 100 | 0 | 0 | 1 |
| Alliance | 6 | 75 | 2 | 25 | 8 |
| SDLP | 2 | 12 | 15 | 88 | 17 |
| Total | 61 | 78 | 17 | 22 | 78 |

**Source:** Compiled from biographies in McAllister, *The 1975 Northern Ireland Convention Election*, Appendix A.

in the Western world. First, the Convention members are disproportionately male; only four of the seventy-eight are women—two
Official Unionists, one DUP member, and one UPNI member. This
proportion (5.2 percent) makes women more numerous in the Convention than in the British House of Commons returned in October
1974 (4.2 percent). Ulster's best known woman politician, Bernadette
Devlin McAliskey, did not contest a seat because she supported the
IRSP boycott of the ballot. In the February 1974 Westminster election in Mid-Ulster she took 25 percent of the vote. In all likelihood,
Bernadette McAliskey would have won a seat in the Convention had
she wished to run.

In age, the Convention members cover a wide range, from Jeremy
Burchill, age twenty-four, to the youthful-seeming seventy-four-year-
old Col. E. H. Brush, an Official Unionist who had a distinguished
record in the British army and is prominent in Down Orange Welfare,
an Ulster paramilitary organization (see Table 8). The two largest
parties—the Loyalists and the SDLP—are the parties that have on
average the youngest politicians. One-quarter of the Loyalist Convention members are under the age of thirty-five, compared to 10
percent in the British House of Commons. None of the SDLP members is over the age of fifty-five, compared to 25 percent in that
more elderly age bracket in Westminster. In aggregate, the Ulster

## Table 8

### COMPARISON OF AGES OF CONVENTION MEMBERS AND WESTMINSTER M.P.s

| | Convention Members | | | | | | West-minster M.P.s (percent) |
|---|---|---|---|---|---|---|---|
| | | | | | Total | | |
| Age | Loyal-ists | UPNI | Alliance/ NILP | SDLP | Number | Percent | |
| Over 65 | 1 | 0 | 1 | 0 | 2 | 3 | 5 |
| 56–65 | 11 | 1 | 1 | 0 | 11 | 14 | 20 |
| 46–55 | 15 | 4 | 3 | 4 | 27 | 35 | 33 |
| 36–45 | 8 | 0 | 4 | 11 | 25 | 32 | 32 |
| Under 35 | 12 | 0 | 0 | 2 | 13 | 17 | 10 |
| Total | 47 | 5 | 9 | 17 | 78 | 100 | 100 |

Source: *The Times Guide to the House of Commons, October, 1974* (London);
Ted Nealon, *Ireland: A Parliamentary Directory, 1973-4* (Dublin: Institute of Public
Administration, 1974); John Harbinson, *The Ulster Unionist Party, 1882-1973*
(Belfast: Blackstaff, 1973); Northern Ireland newspapers.

## Table 9
## COMPARISON OF THE OCCUPATIONS OF
## CONVENTION MEMBERS AND WESTMINSTER M.P.s

| | Convention Members | | | | | | West-minster M.P.s (percent) |
|---|---|---|---|---|---|---|---|
| | | | | | Total | | |
| Occupation | Loyal-ists | UPNI | Alliance/NILP | SDLP | Number | Percent | |
| Professional (including clerics) | 15 | 0 | 5 | 10 | 30 | 38 | 48 |
| Business | 11 | 4 | 3 | 4 | 22 | 28 | 20 |
| Farmers, miscellaneous white collar | 11 | 1 | 1 | 0 | 13 | 17 | 18 |
| Manual workers | 10 | 0 | 0 | 3 | 13 | 17 | 14 |

Source: As in Table 8, and D. E. Butler and Dennis Kavanagh, *The British General Election of October, 1974* (London: Macmillan, 1975), p. 215. British figures refer only to the 609 M.P.s who belong to the three largest parties.

Convention members are younger than their British parliamentary counterparts.

In occupational terms, the membership of the Northern Ireland Convention is more nearly a cross-section of the population of the Province than the Westminster House of Commons is of Britain's. Both assemblies, like their counterparts in other Western nations, are disproportionately middle class. (See Table 9.)

The Ulster Convention has more manual workers in it than the British House of Commons, and its representation of professional people is less biased toward the high-income professions: two-fifths of its thirty professionals are school teachers and clerics, as against one-sixth of the professionals at Westminster, where barristers or university teachers predominate in the professional ranks. The largest group in the Convention, the Loyalists, is the most representative in occupational terms: ten Loyalist Convention members are manual workers and another nine are farmers, the two major occupational groups in the Province.[6] Although the Loyalists do not aim their appeal primarily at labor, they have more manual workers in their ranks in the Convention than the SDLP, which has only three, and almost as high a proportion as the British Parliamentary Labour party

[6] The Loyalists are also more nearly a cross-section of the Province occupationally than the old Unionist party. See Harbinson, *Ulster Unionist Party*, p. 109.

**Table 10**

COMPARISON OF THE EDUCATION OF
CONVENTION MEMBERS AND WESTMINSTER M.P.s

| | Convention Members | | | | | | West-minster M.P.s Oct. 1974 |
| | | | | | Total | | |
| Education | Loyalists | UPNI | Alliance/ NILP | SDLP | Number | Percent | |
|---|---|---|---|---|---|---|---|
| University/ higher | 16 | 0 | 6 | 10 | 32 | 41 | 62 |
| Secondary | 29 | 4 | 3 | 7 | 43 | 55 | 32 |
| Elementary only | 2 | 1 | 0 | 0 | 3 | 4 | 5 |

**Source:** As for Table 9.

(28 percent). The SDLP is distinctive because six of its seventeen members are schoolteachers and another, John Hume, is an ex-teacher. By comparison, only 12 percent of British Labour M.P.s are schoolteachers.

In educational terms, Convention members are less exclusive than their British counterparts (see Table 10). First, the proportion of Westminster M.P.s who are university graduates is half again greater than the Northern Ireland proportion.[7] The median Ulster Convention member completed his education at a secondary school; the median British M.P. is a university graduate. Second, Ulster education is less "exclusive" than its English counterpart. The distinction between fee-paying boarding schools and state schools is far less important in Northern Ireland than it has been in English public life, and nearly all the university graduates have attended Queen's University, Belfast. The largest party, the Loyalists, combines a substantial proportion of university graduates with an even larger proportion of members with a more typical secondary education. Ironically, it is the Social Democratic and Labour party that contributes a disproportionate number of university graduates—though its leader, Gerry Fitt, is a former merchant seaman and not a graduate. Six of the Convention members received at least part of their education in the Republic. Two SDLP members, John Hume and Frank Feeley, studied at Maynooth, a seminary for priests. Four Loyalists—Brian Faulkner,

[7] Convention members are, in educational terms, more like members of the Dublin Dail, for the 20th Dail, 40 percent had a higher education, 53 percent had a secondary education, and 8 percent only an elementary education. Figures calculated from Nealon, *Parliamentary Directory.*

Jim Kilfedder, Kennedy Lindsay, and Ernest Baird—attended secondary school in the Republic or Trinity College, Dublin.

Political experience is the most relevant of all types of experience for those drafting a constitution. Of the Convention members, two-thirds sat in the 1973 Assembly and thus had at least four months' exposure to the problems of governing Northern Ireland. One-quarter sat in the old Stormont Parliament, and five have sat or are concurrently sitting in the British House of Commons. The Loyalists had the largest number of novices in their ranks, twenty out of forty-seven members. This inevitably happens to a party gaining ground. It also reflects the ravages of half a decade of infighting among Unionists and Protestants (see Table 11). The rapid turnover of former Unionists is illustrated by the fact that only nine of the Convention members elected by Loyalists had sat in the old Stormont, as against all five of the UPNI members, five SDLP members, and two additional non-Loyalist members. The large number of novices in Loyalist ranks can cause difficulties, for they are required both to accustom themselves to parliamentary-type procedures *and* to draft a new constitution for their Province, all in a matter of months.

### Table 11
### THE POLITICAL EXPERIENCE OF CONVENTION MEMBERS

| | Previous Service In: | | | | |
| | Assembly | Old Stormont | West-minster | Novices | Total Members |
|---|---|---|---|---|---|
| Loyalists | | | | | |
| Official Unionists | 12 | 6 | 2 | 7 | 19 |
| DUP | 6 | 2 | 1 | 5 | 12 |
| VUP | 6 | 1 | 1 | 8 | 14 |
| Independent Unionists | 2 | 0 | 0 | 0 | 2 |
| Subtotal | 27 | 9 | 4 | 20 | 47 |
| UPNI | 5 | 5 | 0[a] | 0 | 5 |
| Alliance | 6 | | 0[a] | 2 | 8 |
| SDLP | 15 | 5 | 1 | 2 | 17 |
| NILP | 1 | 1 | 0 | 0 | 1 |
| Total | 54 | 21 | 5 | 24 | 78 |

[a] Plus one member each in House of Lords at Westminster.

In Northern Ireland, political experience can be gained in extra-parliamentary and extraconstitutional politics, as well as in parliamentary politics. Any record of the activities of Convention members is likely to be incomplete in this respect, for while some may boast of their previous exploits or current connections with paramilitary groups, others are coy about such matters in campaign biographies. Among the Loyalist candidates, reports indicated that eight to ten Protestant Convention members are linked with various paramilitary organizations, including the Ulster Defence Association, the Ulster Special Constabulary Association, Down Orange Welfare, and the UVF.[8] Another Loyalist Convention member was arrested and charged with carrying a pistol and ammunition in suspicious circumstances a week after the election. Two SDLP members have had their names linked with Catholic "defense" activities. Three Convention members have in the past received jail sentences or been interned for political activities. The eight members of the SDLP who were involved in civil rights activities had thereby gained experience in extraparliamentary protest activities. A substantial number of Orangemen in the Loyalist ranks are also experienced in "marching for a cause." Overall, more members of the Convention have been exposed to political groups prepared to challenge laws than have had experience in "normal" politics in the British Parliament at Westminster, or even in the old Stormont Parliament.

Except in their political experience, Convention members do not differ greatly from members of representative assemblies in other countries. If anything, they more nearly reflect the social characteristics of their constituents than do the professional university-educated M.P.s who predominate in the British House of Commons and, even more, dominate decision making in the British cabinet. What is distinctive about the Convention members is the task before them: to write a constitution, rather than to operate established institutions. They also differ from their political colleagues in more fortunate lands in the magnitude of the problem facing them. To resolve the problems of Northern Ireland, neither education nor youthful liveliness is enough.[9]

---

[8] See, for example, "Para-Military Threat," *Alliance* (the newspaper of the Alliance party), June 1975, and "Politicians or Para-militaries?" *Hibernia* (Dublin), 3 October 1975.

[9] When the author was first researching Ulster politics, he was introduced to a senior (and since defeated) member of the Stormont Parliament. The politician commented, "I hope you have a treble first to deal with this place!" (The reference to high academic distinction in a British university might loosely be translated in American as "You'll need *three* Ph.D.s to understand what's happening here.")

# 6

# IN SEARCH OF A SETTLEMENT

*It would surely be better, Mr. Speaker, to give up not only a part, but if necessary, even the whole, of our Constitution, to preserve the remainder.*

Sir Boyle Roche in Parliament at Dublin, c. 1790

*The air is thick with political impossibilities.*

*Irish Times,* 17 September 1975

The seventy-eight members of the Northern Ireland Convention started with at least one thing in common: a strong desire to resolve political differences by discussions among elected representatives rather than by gun battles among the many armed forces within the Province. The institutions of representative government give elected politicians their influence and legitimacy. A settlement obtained in debate and negotiation confirms the status of conventional party politicians; resolving differences by force is a repudiation of their position.

## Strategic Options

Settlement implies three elements: a *document* setting out the constitutional forms by which Northern Ireland is to be governed in the future, a *deal* dividing the political benefits among all who support the document, and, once this has been agreed upon, a *defense force* strong enough to withstand attacks from the armed opposition that is bound to challenge any majority agreement in a land doomed to government without consensus. Given the plethora of armed forces operating in the Province, Convention politicians placed highest priority on the elaboration of a document or a deal that might produce institutions worth defending.

The votes of the Northern Ireland electorate established a base line for politicking within the Convention, but popular votes are not automatically translated into laws or Convention recommendations. This can only happen through the decisions of elected representatives. The Convention had an inauspicious start. The clearly expressed views of individual Ulstermen had produced a collective body where discord, not harmony, predominated, because of the mutually exclusive positions to which different groups appeared to be pledged.

In accordance with the result of the vote, the parties were represented at the bargaining table in unequal numbers. The Loyalists of the UUUC entered the negotiations with an unambiguous majority of votes, but their constitutional proposals were not accepted by those defeated in the election, a category that included the British government as well as the SDLP. The three pro-British and pro-power-sharing parties—Alliance, UPNI, and Northern Ireland Labour—stood between the two largest blocs in the Convention, without enough votes to make their consent a condition of majority approval for any measure, but with a sufficient following to make their support potentially significant: to be effective, the constitution would require more than a majority, if less than a totality, of popular support. The SDLP retained its monopoly claim to represent Catholics, but it secured only one-fifth of the seats in the Convention, less than the quarter or third usually required to block constitutional reforms in other lands.

**The Range of Possibilities.** Upon entering the Convention, each political group could, if it looked ahead, see an extreme range of possible outcomes, from the maximum desired through the minimum acceptable and, beyond that, to the worst it dreaded coming to pass. At most, the Loyalist Coalition could hope to present constitutional recommendations in so reasonable a manner that they would secure not only the votes of its forty-seven members, but also support from the Alliance, UPNI, and NILP members of the Convention. Negotiations with the SDLP might not change the views of that minority, but the appearance of SDLP intransigence might force the parties in the middle to come off the fence on the Loyalist side, isolating the SDLP. At a minimum, the UUUC wished to keep its uneasy coalition together, thus ensuring an unambiguous majority vote in the Convention for the proposals which it had announced prior to the election. The fear of Loyalists close to Protestant paramilitary organizations was that the efforts of elected representatives might be undermined by a sudden and violent move from those with the ability to destroy, but not to create, civil government.

The Alliance party (and, less significantly, the UPNI and the NILP) hoped that its center position might enable it to bridge the gap between the UUUC and the SDLP. The Alliance and the UPNI agreed with the Loyalists on many specifics, such as policing British sovereignty and skepticism about the Republic of Ireland's role in Ulster. And they agreed with the SDLP about the principle of power sharing. At a minimum, the center parties had to avoid becoming a "me too" voice, appearing merely to echo the Loyalist or the SDLP line. Because they were not the major spokesmen for either community, these parties wished most of all to avoid Protestant-Catholic polarization, which would leave them in a political no-man's land where they could be shot at from both sides.

The SDLP had the widest range of prospects of any party. At one extreme, if its (and the British government's) proclaimed commitment to power sharing could be realized, its leaders would return to office, from which they had been ejected a year previously by the Ulster Workers' Council strike. The past behavior of the British government meant, however, that the SDLP could not count on British support in every eventuality. At a minimum, the SDLP sought to avoid being isolated in the Convention and having to cast its seventeen votes against a document endorsed by the sixty-one votes of the other six parties. The SDLP faced two totally unacceptable but empirically possible threats to its aims. The Provisional IRA could make negotiations impossible by returning to an all-out campaign of violence, or a deal between Loyalists and the British government could return power to Protestant hands, leaving the IRA the only immediately effective opponent of a pro-Loyalist settlement.

While paramilitary groups are not directly represented in the Convention, the decisions they make influence what the elected representatives can and cannot do. The Provisional IRA was not interested in whether the Convention succeeded, but in whether the suspension of its own military activities might lead the British government to make major concessions toward the IRA's goal of the withdrawal of Britain from all parts of the island of Ireland. Concurrently, the IRA kept its weapons well oiled in anticipation of the resumption of its military campaign or the outbreak of sectarian war between Protestants and Catholics. The IRA's SDLP critics charged it with contemplating a return to violence if the Convention succeeded in arriving at a power-sharing formula—that is, with attempting to veto by force a peaceful settlement not in accord with IRA wishes.

Protestant paramilitary organizations had more grounds to hope for a settlement from the Convention. Not only did the Loyalists have a majority there, but also a number of Convention members were linked with a variety of Protestant paramilitary groups. Protestant paramilitants differed among themselves in their patience with and trust in the Convention deliberations. Some were prepared to wait longer than others for a settlement without recourse to force or intimidation. While awaiting the outcome of the Convention, they could deliberate among themselves about questions that uniquely concerned them, such as where to strike—at the Catholic minority, the Republic of Ireland, or the British government—if developments in the Convention did not proceed satisfactorily.

The British and Irish governments could contemplate both ideal and wholly unsatisfactory outcomes of the Convention. The nominal sovereign power, Britain, was temporarily out of the limelight, with no public policy. ("Do you think we ought to have a policy?" inquired a civil servant, when asked where Britain stood. Britain hoped for a compromise between Protestants and Catholics that would save it from having to put forward its own policy or to continue direct rule indefinitely. It feared that the Convention might present a clear majority vote for a legally practicable constitution recommending majority, and thus Loyalist, rule. Britain was on record as disapproving this, because it assumed that the Catholic minority would thereby be excluded from the cabinet. The Irish government was unambiguously committed to supporting Ulster Catholics. It hoped that the Convention could find a compromise acceptable to both the Catholic SDLP and the Loyalists, thus eliminating the need for any action or risk on its part. Failing that, Dublin hoped that the British government would stand by its earlier commitment to continue direct rule rather than return government to a Protestant majority. Both governments feared, as the ultimate in their undoing, that politics might move from Stormont to the streets and country lanes of Ulster, with local armed groups proving more than a match for the security forces mustered by the two states that claim sovereignty over Northern Ireland.

The advertisements of the British government that publicized the Convention to the Ulster electorate were full of negative statements: a convention is *not* a parliament or an assembly; it has *no* government or opposition parties; it does *not* make laws; it is *not* responsible for administering the general services of Northern Ireland.[1] But the British government left vague the positive responsibil-

---

[1] See, for example, *Irish News*, 13 March 1975.

ity of the Convention: "to consider what provision for the government of Northern Ireland is likely to command the most widespread acceptance throughout the whole community." This statutory formulation of the purpose of the Convention was noteworthy because it did not use the word "power sharing," which had been employed in the earlier British government White Paper about the Convention. In other words, the British government had left a statutory loophole enabling it to reject its own plan for the Convention if it subsequently wished to do so.

**A Document or a Deal?** The Convention met for the first time on 8 May in the traditional debating chamber at Stormont, remodelled so that representatives were seated around a half-oval, rather than facing each other confrontation-style as the M.P.s are in the oblong debating chamber of Westminster. The chairman, Sir Robert Lowry, the ranking judge in the Province, quickly established himself as trusted by all sides in the Convention. The British government made clear that it would refrain from any direct efforts to influence the Convention even though it governed the Province from Stormont Castle, only 100 yards from the parliament building where the Convention members met. The procedures for the Convention were left to the members to decide, not without some wrangling.

In the first substantive debate of the Convention in mid-June, seventy-six of its seventy-eight members declared their common, albeit very general, hope that

> this Convention commits itself to devising a system of government for Northern Ireland which will have most widespread acceptance throughout the community; declares its abhorence of violence from all sources and looks forward to open political negotiations within the Convention.[2]

The resolution took for granted a settlement within Northern Ireland, that is, political power should be devolved from Westminster and independent of Dublin. It spoke of Northern Ireland as a single community, which it must be for purposes of government, especially the maintenance of law and order. The members endorsed negotiations about their political differences, rather than a politics of confrontation involving the assertion of mutually exclusive claims.

The crucial question facing the Convention, and particularly the Loyalist majority, was whether to give priority to a document or a deal. A document could set out in black and white specific propositions to be incorporated into a British act of Parliament that would

---

[2] Northern Ireland Constitutional Convention, *Report of Debates* (Belfast: Her Majesty's Stationery Office, 18 June 1975), Column 251.

serve henceforth as a written constitution for self-government in the Province. But without some kind of deal with the SDLP, or at least with Alliance and the UPNI, such a document might never secure approval at Westminster. Even if it did, there was no telling whether it would last a half-century, like the act that established the Stormont Parliament in 1921, or collapse within a matter of months, like the 1973 British-sponsored Assembly Act. A convention concerned primarily with drawing up a constitutional document would concentrate upon matters that particularly demanded the expertise of lawyers. But this expertise was not in great supply in the Convention—or, one might add, in Westminster: the British government's attempts at writing constitutions for colonies approaching independence in the preceding two decades had led to a series of quickly repudiated failures. Allowance was made, however, for members of the Convention to travel to Continental countries that had avoided political discord in spite of their internal divisions, such as the Netherlands and Switzerland.

A deal between the principal parties in the Convention, the UUUC and the SDLP, promised the surest guarantee that the British government would enact into law whatever the Convention recommended. Moreover, it extended the hope that the government established thereby would be supported by a sufficient number of people in the Province to sustain itself against challenges from either Republican or Loyalist armed groups. The incentive for politicians who had recently fought each other to come to an agreement was clear and potent: the promise of office. One difficulty, however, was that an ad hoc agreement between politicians to share office would produce a written constitution as transitory as the political alliance among the individuals named therein. A constitution must endure after individuals, parties, and particular coalitions of interests have passed from the scene. In 1973, the Faulkner Unionists and the SDLP had been able to concentrate upon a political deal to share out offices because a constitution had already been enacted. After this proved short-lived, the British government reversed its priorities. It sought agreement about a constitution, stipulating this document as a necessary condition of any politician securing office thereafter. (The members of the Convention, anxious for office, floated the idea that the Convention could turn itself into a duly constituted assembly without reelection.) A second difficulty was that any deal agreed to by representatives of different parties might stretch to the breaking point the bond between the representatives and those who had elected them, insofar as it was inconsistent with the manifesto pledges with which they had secured their seats.

In the event, the Convention parties decided to do what they knew best how to do: seek a political deal. Instead of establishing committees to examine different types of alternative constitutional arrangements within and outside the United Kingdom, the business committee of the Convention avoided lengthy public debates about constitutional alternatives, after the opening sessions in which each elected member had had an opportunity to air his views, and procedures were agreed. The Convention met for nineteen afternoon sessions in the nine weeks up to 3 July, then adjourned for a July holiday; it did not sit again until 11 September.

## A Productive Recess

With Irish irony, political activity intensified upon the formal adjournment of the Convention. First of all, the chief Convention parties sought to ensure that the unstable coalition that each represented would remain intact—or at least would avoid giving open evidence of major divergences. This was no easy matter, for the Loyalist Coalition contained within its ranks independent personalities such as Ian Paisley and William Craig, as well as three separate parties. The smaller SDLP was divided to a lesser extent than the Loyalist Coalition by personalities and by differences of interest between Catholic representatives in East Ulster, who had most to fear from a Protestant backlash, and representatives from constituencies closer to the border with the Republic of Ireland. The relative weakness of the SDLP in terms of votes made its members understandably more nervous about what might come to pass should a deal fall through.

The second factor making Stormont a center of activity during the Convention recess was the two sides' need to sound each other out about the prospect of a deal leading to a Convention report endorsed by both the UUUC and the SDLP. In the dining rooms, bars, and corridors of Stormont, individuals, sometimes known for conflicting political views, had opportunities to put their heads together for a "wee word." In addition, formal channels for interparty talks were established, involving a variety of bilateral discussions between groups in the Convention. The principal channel for interparty talks was a UUUC-SDLP committee, consisting of William Craig, VUP, William Beattie, DUP, and Austin Ardill, Official Unionist, for the Loyalists; and John Hume, Austin Currie, and Paddy Devlin for the SDLP. Since the participants in the interparty talks had to report back to their own colleagues, intraparty talks moved forward concurrently with interparty discussions during the Convention recess.

**A Violent Truce.** Convention members closeted with each other in search of a settlement could not isolate themselves from events around them. As the summer moved on, these events increasingly emphasized the difficulty of securing trust and agreement among all the parties to the dispute.

The actions of the British government in Northern Ireland unintentionally produced a kind of negative consensus among Convention members. However much they differed in what they were for, they agreed that direct rule of the Province by the British government was unacceptable, even dangerous. The root of the trouble was the belief that the British put more trust in talking with gunmen than in talking with elected public representatives. Originally based on the British failure to cope with the UWC strike in May 1974, this perception was confirmed by Britain's negotiations with the Provisional IRA, which led to a truce on 10 February 1975. The British rationale for entering such discussions was summed up by an anonymous British civil servant: "The paramilitary figures of today are the politicians of tomorrow." [3]

The truce gave the Provisional IRA official British recognition, because incident centers were established through which British officials and representatives of Sinn Fein (the political wing of the Provisional Republican movement) could negotiate on hot-line telephones in efforts to prevent incidents from escalating into riots. Sinn Fein advertised twenty incident centers in Catholic newspapers and sought to use these centers as focal points for political activity within the Catholic community. Meanwhile, the Provisional IRA could use the respite occasioned by the truce to rearm and regroup, and the release of men interned for alleged Republican activities provided it with additional trained manpower. The negotiations did not induce either side to eschew the use of force and, taken together, their statements about the truce conjured up an almost *Catch-22* situation. The Belfast Brigade of the IRA declared: "The level of our activity will at all times be related to the activity of the British occupation and RUC forces." The Northern Ireland Office meanwhile announced: "The level of activity by the Army and the Police will be related to the level of violence." [4]

SDLP members were furious with the recognition that the British government had given to the Provisional IRA, when the SDLP was the only legitimately elected representative body in the Catholic community. Paddy Devlin accused Merlyn Rees, the British secretary of state, of trying to wreck the Convention created by an election his

---

[3] "Murder at Bogus Checkpoint," The *Times* (London), 26 August 1975.

[4] Both quotations from "Wit and Wisdom," *Alliance* (Belfast), September 1975.

office had sanctioned. Devlin concluded, "Mr. Rees is engaged in a kind of perversion of logic, common sense and reason which the English like to think of as typically Irish."[5]

Loyalists were infuriated by British actions too, for they feared that the truce had occurred only because the British government had secretly agreed to withdraw from the Province, since British withdrawal is the ultimate aim of Republicans. The Loyalists' distrust was fueled by a statement in mid-May by the Rev. William Arlow, a Belfast Protestant clergyman acting as an intermediary in the truce talks. Arlow said that he had reason to believe that the British would begin their withdrawal following the failure of the Convention. The British government promptly denied this and also denied subsequent leaks about an alleged British-Provisional IRA understanding. Protestants paid less attention to the leaks than to the fact that the IRA was no longer under pressure from the British army or regularly attacking British soldiers. Thanks to a leak from British army sources, Ian Paisley produced an army document that said a Belfast leader of the Provisional IRA was not now a wanted man to be arrested on sight and charged that the police had avoided detaining this man when an opportunity had arisen. When Protestant-Catholic sectarian murders intensified in the South Armagh border area in August, the British army headquarters, Lisburn, issued a statement on 25 August 1975 that effectively surrendered any claim to maintaining security there after dark: "People are advised to travel during daylight hours, and only use the main, authorised roads and crossing points." Loyalist Convention members were also angered that Northern Ireland Office officials were ready to find time to meet delegations of Protestant paramilitary groups, including organizations that had been declared illegal, while simultaneously claiming that they had neither the time nor the need to meet elected Loyalist members of the Convention to discuss the problems of the Province.

By the end of August, the Convention members' distrust of the British government had become so severe that criticisms voiced anonymously to a *Sunday Times* journalist might have come from either the Loyalist or the SDLP ranks: "Merlyn Rees has got to choose between the ballot box and the power of a gun barrel. So far he is trying to deal with both, which is a recipe for disaster."[6]

Amidst the political uncertainties, one thing was patently clear: the truce involving the British army and the Provisional IRA had

---

[5] See "Letters to the Editor," *New Statesman* (London), 19 September 1975.

[6] See "Ulster: Rees Stops Troop Rundown," *Sunday Times* (London), 31 August 1975.

failed to reduce the death toll in the Province. In the first nine months following the truce, 196 people lost their lives in political violence. This total was 37 more than had been killed in the equivalent period in 1974 when no truce had been in effect. The dead included 5 people killed in a bomb attack on a public house used by Loyalists on the Shankill Road, Belfast, a Protestant worker killed after being mobbed in the Catholic Lower Falls area of Belfast when delivering building materials to repair bomb-damaged homes there, 3 members of the Dublin-based Miami Showband murdered by the UVF in South Down when returning from an engagement, 5 people killed when Republicans fired automatic weapons into an Orange Hall at Tullyvallen, South Armagh, while a meeting was in progress, and 11 who died on 2 October, a day of UVF-sponsored violence in protest against Republican-sponsored violence in the preceding weeks.

During the so-called truce, the pattern of violence shifted significantly. Republican gunmen concentrated upon shooting individual Protestants, rather than making more or less random bomb attacks. Protestant armed groups, their fears of a Republican takeover heightened by the truce, continued to maintain their status as the more deadly of the paramilitary communities. The chief beneficiaries of the truce have been the security forces, particularly the British army, which lost only eight men in the first nine months of the truce compared to twenty-two killed in this period in the previous year.

The British government viewed the violence during the truce phlegmatically. One senior civil servant at Stormont Castle commented, apropos Protestant and Catholic demands for more effective security measures, "In this place, crises come and crises go. This is just one of many which we do not recognize as a crisis. We see this whole thing as a ten-round contest of which we've just reached the end of round three." [7] An Ulster journalist explained British phlegm less kindly:

> The only group which is clearly coming out ahead in the truce is the British Army, which is suffering fewer casualties. It is surely a chilling innovation when military sophistication reaches a point where it is the military who stay alive and the civilians who do the dying.[8]

In a radio broadcast on 31 August, British Secretary of State Merlyn Rees sought to reassure nervous Ulstermen by stating, "For us to abdicate our responsibilities in Northern Ireland would lead to a

---

[7] "How Despair Brings Hope," *Sunday Times* (London), 7 September 1975.

[8] Michael McKeown, "Killings during the Ceasefire," *Hibernia* (Dublin), 3 October 1975.

Congo-type situation, and I am convinced that this would inevitably lap over into Britain." Northern Ireland listeners could not help but note that this argument showed concern for their safety only insofar as it affected people in Britain.

As the death toll mounted in spite of the truce, both Protestant and Catholic politicians became increasingly nervous and unsettled. The British government seemed unable or, even worse, unwilling to take military action in the face of brutal sectarian killings. SDLP members of the Convention met with the British secretary of state in late August to demand an investigation into the activities of named members of the Ulster Defence Regiment. In several vicious sectarian murders, gunmen had posed in UDR uniforms while carrying out their work. The secretary of state declared the UVF an illegal organization following its admission of responsibility for a day of violence in which eleven people died in early October—but it did this only after negotiations with representatives of the UVF had shown ·that the group's terms for a truce were "unreasonable." The Northern Ireland Office admitted that the truce with the IRA had been made "a mockery and a travesty" by events, but nonetheless regarded it as "an opportunity to return to a more normal way of life." [9] Loyalist Convention members, despairing of the British government, looked elsewhere for support. A Vanguard member of the Westminster Parliament, the Rev. Robert Bradford, declared:

> It may well become necessary, in the light of further British ineptitude, for the politicians to ask the RUC, the Reservists and the UDR to form a disciplined army to meet the avalanche of IRA horror. We may well have to become "Queen's rebels" in order to remain subjects of any kind.[10]

Another Loyalist, Ernest Baird, deputy leader of Vanguard, declared, "There is a credibility gap of Lyndon Johnson proportions in that the people in the street just don't believe the Government anymore." [11]

The frustrations of both Loyalist and SDLP representatives during the summer gave a positive impetus to private discussions between the three-man negotiating teams of the UUUC and the SDLP. The negotiators agreed upon the importance of returning self-government to Northern Ireland because of dissatisfaction with the operation of direct rule. They also agreed upon the desirability of seeking a deal

---

9 "Rees and IRA Agree Truce of Words Holds," *The Guardian* (London), 25 September 1975.

10 "Want RUC to be Loyalist 'Soldiers,' " *Irish Times*, 29 August 1975.

11 "Probe UDR Link with Loyalists, Rees Told," *Irish News*, 28 August 1975.

through face-to-face negotiations without the involvement of representatives of Britain or the Irish Republic. Progress in the negotiations was sufficiently promising that the recall of the Convention originally fixed for 19 August was postponed until mid-September.

**The Loyalist Negotiating Document.** On 26 August 1975, the three Loyalist negotiators submitted to SDLP representatives a negotiating document approved by the UUUC setting out proposals for an agreed Convention report. After repeating the manifesto declaration that "the traditional British democratic parliamentary system is essentially the right one," the paper expanded upon the important role of parliamentary committees under opposition chairmanship. In a departure from the principle of majority rule, the UUUC proposed that the opposition should have the same number of members as the governing party on each committee. In addition, the UUUC offered two negotiating points not explicit in its spring manifesto. One was the creation of a special Security Committee under opposition chairmanship to scrutinize government security policy during periods of emergency. Second, in outlining the theoretical circumstances in which multiparty government (that is, coalition or power sharing) might come about, it added, after references to electoral pacts or the absence of a single party with a majority of seats, "where an emergency or crisis situation exists and parties by agreement come together in the national interest for the duration of the crisis." This crucial clause did not depart from the Loyalist assertion that power sharing had no place in a constitutional document. It offered, without constitutional guarantees, the prospect of a deal that would give office to the SDLP forthwith if it accepted the institutions that the Loyalists proposed.[12]

More interested in a deal than a document, the SDLP responded promptly, albeit guardedly, to the Loyalist proposals. It based its negotiating position upon parameters laid down in the British government's 1974 White Paper, especially power sharing. Its five points for negotiation were: the return of police powers to the Province, the form of power sharing, institutionalized cooperation between the governments in Belfast and Dublin, endorsement of any deal by a referendum within Northern Ireland, and a request to the Republic to give full support to these institutions by a referendum. It reaffirmed that an enhanced role in parliamentary committee work would be insufficient to meet the SDLP's demand for participation in government: It

---

[12] For the full text of these negotiating documents and subsequent recommendations and reports from parties in the Convention, see *Draft Reports Submitted under Rule 16(1)* (Belfast: Northern Ireland Convention, 20 October 1975).

welcomed the UUUC reference to the prospect of voluntary coalition in the face of the crisis conditions obtaining in Northern Ireland and sought "more information as to UUUC thinking on this point." [13] The members of the two negotiating teams proceeded to consult with the chairman of the Convention and his staff to explore ways in which agreement might be advanced—methods by which an emergency crisis might be proclaimed, for example, and a coalition government given the sanction of popular endorsement.

**The Defeat of William Craig.** In conducting interparty negotiations, the Vanguard leader, William Craig, took the initiative in the Loyalist camp. The ideas that Craig associated himself with were not new, though draped in novel circumlocutions to avoid association with old anathemas. They had been circulating privately in the corridors of the Convention for months. What was new was their appearance in an official UUUC document, endorsed by a man with Craig's reputation for denouncing minority aspirations. Craig had been the minister of home affairs who had declared illegal the initial civil rights march at Londonderry on 5 October 1968; this had resulted in the confrontation between police and demonstrators that had stimulated subsequent demonstrations throughout the Province. In a talk in London in October 1972, he had said, "I am prepared to come out and shoot to kill." Shortly after the successful UWC strike, Craig declared, "If there is no other way to achieve the sort of Constitution to maintain the heritage we believe in we will wage civil war in the fullest sense of the word." Ten days after the Convention election, the Vanguard leader had interpreted the outcome thus: "The idea of any power-sharing with Republicans is as dead as a dodo." [14]

Craig's hard-line credentials were vouched for by the institutions of the Vanguard movement, which brought Craig into regular contact with leaders of major Protestant paramilitary bodies. On 6 September the Ulster Loyalist Central Co-ordinating Committee, embracing representatives of most Protestant paramilitary bodies, endorsed continued negotiations within the Convention to secure the return of self-government to the Province. The Loyalist paramilitary groups justified this as the best means of once again placing responsibility for internal security in the hands of Ulstermen.

---

[13] Ibid., p. 39.
[14] All quotations from "The Inside Information that 'Converted' Bill Craig," *Sunday Times* (London), 14 September 1975, a sympathetic portrait of the Ulster politician.

The unity of the Loyalists in support of Craig's negotiations lasted for only two weeks. Formally, the issue that led the majority of Loyalists to part from Craig seemed to be a matter of theological detail: the interpretation of the final clause in the UUUC-endorsed document of 26 August accepting coalition government on a voluntary basis in times of crisis. The May manifesto had neither explicitly endorsed this condition nor explicitly rejected it. It had only rejected compulsory power sharing as in the 1973 Assembly Act. Craig argued that an emergency coalition would not be compulsory power sharing because it would be based upon voluntary consent that could be withdrawn by the Loyalist majority as and when it wished. Craig held that if the British government stood firm against accepting any Convention proposals not agreed to by the SDLP, this would constitute an emergency justifying voluntary coalition. (SDLP members warily noted that a voluntary coalition could break up, leaving them out in the cold, with the Loyalists enjoying the constitutional powers of a government that could quickly come to resemble the old Stormont regime.) Craig was prepared to interpret the SDLP's readiness to take office within a Northern Ireland government as sufficient evidence that the party's aspiration for a Council of Ireland did not make it Republican, a label that would prevent Loyalists from working with the SDLP members. The manifesto was silent about the Republican or non-Republican status of the SDLP; this was to be left open for negotiation. Not least in importance, Craig undoubtedly differed from other prominent figures in the UUUC about who should inherit the chief political position within an emergency coalition. If the negotiations succeeded, he clearly saw himself, rather than Harry West or Ian Paisley, as the man on top.

One thing promptly became clear: William Craig had failed to assess accurately the temper of his colleagues in the UUUC. Within eight weeks of identifying himself so closely with the idea of an emergency coalition that included the SDLP, William Craig was expelled from membership in the UUUC. Ian Paisley, leader of the Democratic Unionist party, promoted the rejection of the initiative that Craig had taken, ostensibly with the support of the entire Loyalist Coalition. A UUUC meeting on 8 September voted thirty-seven to one to reject sharing office with Republicans in any future government of Northern Ireland. The SDLP was bracketed in the Republican category during the debate. The resolution, as SDLP critics were ready to point out, was at variance with the proposals of 26 August, which had recognized three different ways in which cabinet office might be shared with the SDLP. It was also said to be at variance with the

Loyalists' manifesto, which had proposed assigning "powerful" parliamentary committee chairmanships to the SDLP. What was indubitably clear amidst charges and countercharges was that Craig had lost any claim to speak for the Loyalist Coalition. On 7 October a special meeting of the United Ulster Unionist Council, attended by representatives of the Orange Order and related bodies as well as by Convention party representatives, denounced Craig's advocacy of "positions in Cabinet for Republicans" as "neither necessary or in keeping with our pledge to the electorate." The statement of the Council closed with a ringing Paisleyite injunction: "The purposes of God may be thwarted, but not for ever." [15] On 23 October, the UUUC Convention members voted twenty-four to zero to expel Craig from their ranks; Vanguard members of the UUUC did not vote.

Within the Vanguard movement in the Convention, William Craig found little support. Nine of the thirteen, including the party's deputy leader, Ernest Baird, refused to endorse Craig's view that "the UUUC have devalued the Convention." [16] The Vanguard majority announced that they would form a group called the Ulster Unionist Movement within the Convention, dedicated to establishing the unity of all the Loyalist parties. Craig's position was stronger within the Vanguard movement outside the Convention. The party's central council endorsed his views by a vote of 128 to 79 at a meeting on 12 October. Of the three Convention members who had initially sided with him in the dispute, two were prominent in paramilitary groups, Glen Barr of the Ulster Defence Association and George Green of the Ulster Special Constabulary Association. Among the paramilitary groups, only the illegal Ulster Volunteer Force openly attacked Craig's stand. One UDA man explained why he supported Craig's negotiated settlement rather than a Loyalist policy of confrontation, saying, "It's all right for the politicians to start the war, but we'll have to fight it." [17] Craig regarded his defeat within the Convention as a temporary setback rather than a rejection of the policy he had promoted.[18]

While the UUUC quarreled about how to treat the Catholic minority, the SDLP remained in the background. It did not need to commit itself to any particular Loyalist initiative until it knew what

---

[15] See "Opponents of Craig Step Up Attack," *Irish Times*, 8 October 1975.

[16] Resignation letter of William Craig, *Irish Times*, 10 September 1975.

[17] "How Craig's Change of Heart Brought the Knives Out," *Irish Times*, 11 September 1975.

[18] For a detailed defense of Craig's actions, see the lengthy account contained in "Paisley Bowed to Pressure—Claim," *Irish Times*, 4 November 1975.

the initiative was, how many Loyalists supported it, and whether the offer was an attempt to secure SDLP cooperation or a tactical move designed to assist one Loyalist faction. The idea of participation in a coalition government, whatever label it bore, was consistent with the SDLP's declared aims. But the meaning of the support given the proposal by Protestant paramilitants was ambiguous. It could mean that the paramilitants were prepared to retire from active service to secure the return of self-government to Northern Ireland from Westminster or it could mean that they were prepared to collaborate with the SDLP temporarily—as long as they retained the right to break up the coalition as and when they wished and return to the traditional form of government by a Protestant majority. As if to remind his followers or himself that his fundamental views had not changed, Craig told a radio interviewer a week after making his proposal, "If anyone tries by force to override the will of the majority in Northern Ireland he will be resisted. We will fight back and fighting back does mean 'shoot to kill.' It doesn't mean dressing up and being toy soldiers." [19] One skeptical civil servant anonymously summed up the situation with characteristic Irish insistence upon the past: "Craig's always been wrong before. Why should he be different now?" In tactical terms, the controversies within the UUUC immediately strengthened the SDLP. The onus for the impasse in the Convention was now placed upon the divided Loyalists rather than upon a recalcitrant minority. "The SDLP has had reasonableness thrust upon them," commented an anonymous observer.

## The Outcome

**The Parties' Reports to the Convention.** The enabling act establishing the Convention required it to produce a report within six months, that is, by 7 November 1975. By mid-September there was no prospect of laboriously putting together a new coalition or credibly restoring the old Loyalist Coalition prior to that statutory deadline. In the midst of the squabbles within the Loyalist ranks, all parties were asked to submit draft reports to the Convention chairman, to be deliberated upon by the Convention as a whole. Five parties did so.[20]

The United Ulster Unionist Coalition presented the fullest document, including a summary of the work of the Convention and factual

---

[19] "Secret Ulster Talks on Craig Move," The *Times* (London), 15 September 1975.
[20] For a summary of the five parties' reports, see *Report of Debates*, 30 September 1975, Cols. 528-33, and the speeches reported thereafter. The statement of the Ulster Dominion Group is not considered here, since Dr. Kennedy Lindsay, a Convention member, is the only known member of his group.

appendices. Its report rejected the idea of institutionalized power sharing as a "disruptive and divisive" plan to "freeze and fossilise the existing party structures and, in a phrase, institutionalize sectarianism in government." [21] Power sharing was thus an unwarranted departure from British standards of parliamentary government. The UUUC constitutional proposals repeated those rehearsed in the preceding months, with two noteworthy exceptions: omission of the paragraph referring to a security committee chaired by an opposition representative and an amended reference to the theoretical possibility of an emergency coalition declaring that such a coalition must be based on conventional principles of British parliamentary government. On the partisan level, the statement widened the distance between the Loyalists and the SDLP by asserting that "the language and attitudes of republicanism still linger" in its ranks and that "the basic thrust of that party is not in the realm of social democratic and labour philosophy but in a desire to take Northern Ireland outside the Union." The UUUC attacked the SDLP for making endorsement of policing in the Province contingent upon SDLP participation in government. "To end the political vacuum and defeat terrorism," it called upon the British government to restore the British style of parliamentary government to Northern Ireland. William Craig and his three Convention supporters did not exercise their right to file a separate report. The seventy-six-clause draft constitution embodying the Loyalist recommendations was noteworthy for entrenching power at Stormont and restricting the British government from interference.

The SDLP proposals, too, emphasized the distance between the SDLP and the UUUC, though they blamed the latter for the failure of the Convention to reach agreement. The SDLP's document began by rejecting the very idea of a report prepared by a single party and endorsed by majority vote. It reaffirmed its preference for a document compiled by the chairman and not subject to a final Convention vote. The SDLP based its case upon the 1974 British White Paper proposing the Convention. That document had emphasized the need for power sharing, an Irish dimension, and Westminster's absolute right to veto what the Convention proposed. The fact that these conditions were not stated in the act establishing the Convention was said to be of little consequence. The SDLP argued that because the Loyalists had refused to accept these "political parameters . . . no fruitful dialogue has yet taken place between the members of the Convention." Because the Loyalists had rejected power sharing in principle, the SDLP

---

[21] For the source of quotation from the reports of the several parties, see *Draft Reports Submitted under Rule 16(1)*.

saw no need to offer detailed plans for implementing power sharing and an institutionalized Irish dimension. The SDLP argued that these institutions had already been set out in Britain's 1973 Assembly Act, the act repudiated by the Ulster Workers' Council strike leading to the Convention. Instead of describing institutions, the SDLP concentrated upon justifying the deal it sought. It said that the crucial issue was power sharing, "whether Northern Ireland is to be governed by a Protestant ascendancy regime or whether it is to become a modern society, the government of which will cherish all the citizens equally." It rejected Loyalist claims that the SDLP was outside the pale of office holding, noting that its members denounced both IRA violence and Protestant paramilitary activity and that its aspiration for the peaceful unification of Ireland opened up the prospect of a constitutional change no greater than that implied by the independent Ulster line of some UUUC members. It declared that the participation of the SDLP in government and governmental cooperation with the Republic could make security within the Province easier to maintain.

The final proposals of the Alliance, UPNI, and Northern Ireland Labour parties echoed their manifesto statements and received little notice; collectively as well as singly, these parties could not dominate a Convention in which Loyalist unity prevailed. The introduction of the Alliance party's proposal to the debate was notable for the praise Bob Cooper, the party's deputy leader, gave the document because it *departed from* British practice. Cooper asserted that "an unjustified sense of inferiority" led Ulstermen "slavishly to copy what is done in the rest of the United Kingdom." He drew attention to the fact that the two-party system of adversary politics that the Loyalists endorsed had increasingly come under criticism in Great Britain in the 1970s.[22] The UPNI recommendations were extremely brief and left vague how "an agreed coalition" (UPNI's euphemism for power sharing) was to be sustained. The NILP document announced: "The Ulster Convention has not failed, nor has it succeeded; it has just commenced its historic task." It saw a voluntary coalition in the face of crisis along Craig's lines as the most desirable immediate arrangement; failing that, it advocated the continuation of direct rule from Britain. In the long run, it looked to "the emergence of new political attitudes and parties which (like the NILP) are based on social and economic interests and not merely on constitutional confrontation."

The positions taken by the parties precluded a unanimous report. Although there was agreement about many things that constitute the

---

[22] See *Report of Debates*, 2 October 1975, Col. 675.

normal stuff of politics, there was less about the real stuff of constitutional controversy in Northern Ireland. The Loyalist statement commented, "The Convention has been unable to agree on fundamentals. In the distress and violence of the times this is hardly surprising." The concluding sessions of the Convention were desultory. William Craig did not use the opportunity of the debates to clarify where he stood in the light of the events of the previous two months. The SDLP avoided pressing votes upon each clause with which it disagreed, so that its minority position would not be emphasized. The center parties also wished to avoid repeated votes, in part because they tended to agree with the UUUC on almost all issues except the crucial one, power sharing, by whatever name it was called. The Loyalist document was approved, forty-two votes to thirty-one. William Craig was among the majority voting for the UUUC anti-power-sharing plan. One anonymous Convention official summed up the session with the comment, "There has been no Convention. We've only had the repetition of set positions by the parties."

The Convention's report could not be the end of politics in Northern Ireland, but merely the conclusion of one more phase in a continuing story of travail. The Convention election was evidence that the majority of voters in the Province would not vote for candidates who recommended power sharing. The late summer negotiations showed that there were elected representatives in both communities who believed that, under another name, voluntary coalition between politicians with some diametrically opposed views was better than any alternative form of government likely to be available to Ulstermen. But the idea of power sharing failed, as it had in 1974, to attract sufficient political support. The split in the Loyalist Coalition offered no immediate advantage to the SDLP because the anti-power-sharing Loyalists retained their absolute majority in the Convention, forty out of seventy-eight members. Moreover, the seven Loyalists outside the Coalition included three who were, if anything, more hard-line than the official leadership, as well as Craig's four Vanguard men. The split in the Loyalist camp did offer the SDLP the longer-term prospect of playing off one part of that coalition against another, particularly since the Official Unionists, the largest single party in the UUUC, were least affected by the polarization between Paisley's party and Craig's group.

**Britain's Dilemma.** In the immediate aftermath, the inability of the Convention to reach agreement returned the political initiative to the British government. Once again, British ministers have had to face the fact that their plans for the future government of Northern Ireland appear unacceptable to a majority of Ulstermen. Since power sharing requires the consent of a majority of the majority, as well as of a majority of the minority, the Loyalists can veto Westminster's wishes. British ministers could canvass three broad alternatives. The first, to legislate at Westminster for the future government of the Province, seems likely to create maximum hostility within Northern Ireland. The second, to refer the report back to the Convention, was technically feasible, for the act establishing the Convention included provisions for prolonging its life past the initial 7 November reporting deadline so that the British government might have elected politicians with whom to negotiate. The British government decided to extend the Convention's life by six months, moving the deadline for "deciding something" to 7 May 1976. This, like the third alternative, a popular referendum within Northern Ireland, begged the question: what could the British government ask the people or the representatives of the people of Northern Ireland to consider that they have not already considered at great length? On what question have they not already registered their views?

The choices confronting British officials are almost as constant as the political situation is volatile. In a volatile situation, the case for a waiting game is weak, even though Britain may think this the best course available. The alternative to consulting once again with elected representatives or the electorate is to base policies upon superior force. The British government has given hostages to fortune by banking so heavily upon a truce with the IRA and a decline in Loyalist-inspired violence during the Convention period. As the Convention moved toward its 7 November report, news from within the Ulster Volunteer Force ranks indicated that some Protestant paramilitants were once again discussing the need for an active campaign to advance their cause. From the Republican side, on 19 October the president of Provisional Sinn Fein, Ruairi O'Bradaigh, declared that British army actions during the truce required violent reprisals by the IRA as steps "necessary to maintain the truce." He added ominously that, in default of further evidence of British disengagement from Northern Ireland, Republicans would "renew the struggle and wrest control from the British government by continuing to make British rule impossible." [23] The opposition party in the Irish Republic, Fianna Fail, stirred up fears too by altering its policy and calling for a British declaration of an "ordered withdrawal from Northern Ireland" as a

---

[23] "O'Bradaigh Confident Force Prevailing for Withdrawal," *Irish Times*, 20 October 1975.

desirable step toward Irish unity.[24] The longer the British government retains responsibility for the security of the Province, the greater its own culpability for the absence of public order.

To test the adherence of the Convention majority to its proposals for majority rule, the British government referred the initial report back for reconsideration on 14 January 1976. It emphasized the importance of providing a form of partnership and participation, and also sought advice about interim institutions that might evolve into a permanent and agreed constitutional settlement. The political parties represented in the Convention once again began a series of interparty talks, but the UUUC majority firmly rejected William Craig's proposal of a voluntary coalition, and the SDLP minority remained firmly committed to its demand for office, a position unacceptable to the Loyalist majority. The Alliance party sought to amend the majority report to offer more to the Catholic minority's representatives, but its efforts failed. In a series of votes on 3 March, the Loyalist majority reaffirmed its recommendations for governing Northern Ireland by a cabinet formed by a majority party as in a British government in London. The British government then announced that the Convention was dissolved, saying that the Convention's recommendations were unlikely to provide a basis for stable government in the Province in the future because a majority government would be exclusively Protestant.

The end of the Convention does not mean the end of politics in Northern Ireland, for the institutions of direct rule continue unaltered in form by the Convention's demise. But the dismissal of the only Ulster representative body gives more attention to nonelected parties to the dispute, the IRA and Protestant paramilitary forces. Their work of destruction continues. In the first two months of 1976, seventy-five people died from political violence within Northern Ireland, primarily as the result of sectarian assassinations. A continuation of such a death rate throughout the year would result in the worst annual total of fatalities since the Troubles commenced in 1969. Even if the monthly rate of murders, shootings, and explosions declines during 1976, neither the British government nor Northern Ireland politicians can point to reasons why the violence should not continue into 1977—or even into the years beyond.

Time is not only against the British government, but also against the people of Northern Ireland; they no longer stand at the crossroads of choice. As one Convention member pointed out: "We have not

---

[24] "Lynch Calls for NI Withdrawal Pledge," *Irish News*, 30 October 1975.

been at the cross-roads. We took the wrong turn and we have been going with ever-increasing speed down the wrong road." [25] The members of the Convention would disagree only about whether the government of Ulster has been on the wrong course for years, for decades, or for centuries.

---

[25] Robert Cooper, Alliance member, *Report of Debates*, 2 October 1975, Col. 677.

# 7
# THE LIMITS OF CHOICE

*It is hard to visualise a situation where the realization of one aspiration does not mean the extinction of another.*

Belfast Telegraph, 9 April 1975

*Northern Ireland One Big Emergency Situation*

Headline, *Irish News*, Belfast, 27 October 1975

## An Insoluble Problem

Many talk about a solution to Ulster's political problem but few are prepared to say what the problem is. The reason is simple. *The problem is that there is no solution*—at least no solution recognizable in those more fortunate parts of the Anglo-American world that are governed with consensus. In such lands disagreements about what government should do are continual, but there is consensus about how the nation is defined and how it should be governed. For example, Americans no longer argue the merits of secession by the South or of an invasion of Canada with the aim of creating a single North American state. Nor do British politicians debate whether the country should be governed by a Parliament, a president, or an absolute monarch. In Northern Ireland, by contrast, political debate concerns the very existence of the state.

Any fool can govern with consensus—and some fools have. Governing without consensus is a different matter. From the time of the Egyptian Pharoahs, governors have exercised authority without the endorsement of popular election. But in the contemporary world, governing without consensus is thought to be undesirable, the last resort of dictators whose acts harm those they govern. Yet government without consensus remains a fact of life in the majority of countries represented in the United Nations. Three-quarters of the U.N. member states are not prepared to entrust to popular election the choice of their rulers, and there is no sign that the proportion is falling.

The immediate need in Northern Ireland is some form of civil government—with or without consensus. Such a government might provide a settlement of only limited or uncertain duration, but it would be a change from the present vacuum. Today, Northern Ireland lacks two basic attributes of the modern state: a constitution and a security organization with an effective claim to a monopoly of force.

Since the Troubles commenced, the British government has authorized four successive sets of institutions: a Unionist party regime at Stormont, direct rule from London, a power-sharing Northern Ireland Executive, and direct rule once again. By calling for the election of a Constitutional Convention, the British government signified that it is looking for yet another change of regime in Northern Ireland—if not to make for the better governance of the Province, at least to relieve London of the burdens of direct rule.

It is clear from a casual stroll around Belfast that the Northern Ireland Office, the nominal locus of authority, is not the effective source of authority. Effective authority belongs to British soldiers, guns at the ready. Such government as Britain provides cannot be described as *civil* government. And the streets and homes of Ulstermen bear witness to the power of other armies, fighting in the name of the IRA or of one or another Protestant paramilitary group. The British army, the Republican armies, and the Protestant paramilitary groups compete with each other. The absence of any monopoly of force, the *sine qua non* of a state, creates a void in place of public order.

Notwithstanding many reversals of British policy since 1969, the British army has been defending regimes that, for all their intermittent ineffectiveness, have at least temporarily existed. By contrast, IRA groups have been fighting for a government that has never existed, a thirty-two-county Republican Ireland. Protestant paramilitants disagree about whether they are seeking a return to the mid-1960s status quo ante or fighting for a new departure in Ulster government. Northern Ireland has a surfeit of men willing to fight or be killed for what they believe in. With authority suspended, it lacks a government worth killing for.

The weakness of many so-called solutions to the Northern Ireland problem is that they are addressed to a problem that is not in fact there or they assume conditions that do not now exist in the Province. Such well-intentioned solutions leave untouched the central political problem of the Province: the absence of civil government. Conceivably, at some future date, the emergence of political differences along class lines, the worldwide unification of the Christian churches, an increase in contact between Protestants and Catholics, or strong leadership from politicians could end the discord that currently prevails. But this has not happened yet. In the 1975 Convention election, the two political parties emphasizing class politics as well as constitutional politics—the Northern Ireland Labour party and the Republican Clubs (supporters of the "Red" Official IRA)—together polled 3.6 percent of the vote. While Catholic Pope, Anglican bishop, and Presbyterian minister can sometimes sit down together in Rome, Protestants and Catholics in Northern Ireland disagree about the very principle of uniting the Protestant and Catholic churches, because both communities expect that such unity would only occur on terms favorable to Catholics. Before the Troubles of 1969, there were many areas of Belfast where Protestants and Catholics lived in the same streets. But it is just these neighborhoods that have been hardest hit by the Troubles, from which more than 10,000 families have been forced to flee as paramilitary groups have sought, by intimidation and force, to secure every street for one religion or the other. Successive British efforts to make Ulster politicians into "strong" leaders by forcing them to act against the wishes of the mass of their voters have led to the downfall of such politicians. For example, Brian Faulkner, head of the British-sponsored power-sharing Executive in 1974, could secure only 10 percent of the first-preference votes in his South Down constituency in the 1975 Convention election. The British government took a strong stand during the Ulster Workers' Council strike in 1974, telling Loyalists what they should do rather than negotiating with them. The firmness that was meant as a token of strength was in fact only a sign of rigidity and was publicly broken by the greater Loyalist strength.

Northern Ireland politicians cannot deal with the problems of the present by hypothesizing that these problems will go away some day. There is not world enough and time. In the brutal arena of Ulster politics, Lord Keynes's dictum, "In the long run, we are all dead," might become, "In the short run, many can be destroyed." The job of an Ulster politician is not to solve problems that he has inherited, but to cope with a situation he finds in front of him. To do this may only be dealing with symptoms. But radical surgery is of no use if the problem is organic and not amenable to surgical

141

treatment. The symptoms, moreover, are disturbing enough. One night of violence provoked by any of the many armed forces operating in the Province can destroy what a politician has been working toward for months, or alternatively it can offer the chance for an initiative which might result in alliances that had hitherto seemed inconceivable.

In many political situations, "wait and see" is a reasonable response to the possibility of future difficulties. Some prophecies of doom will never come to pass, and others will materialize in unanticipated forms. Often the only thing that will be lost by delaying action is money. But in Northern Ireland, the one thing that is sure to be lost is human life. The number of deaths by political violence tabulated in Table 1 is unfortunately not a final total, but only an account of deaths to date.

To make government unworkable is relatively easy, as the civil rights demonstrations of 1968–69, the IRA military campaign of 1971–72, and the Ulster Workers' Council strike of 1974 demonstrate. To make a regime work without consensus is far more difficult. In the troubled state of Northern Ireland, a regime must not only have the force of authority, leading fully allegiant citizens to comply with its basic laws. It must also have the authority of force to make those who do not wish to do so comply with its laws. Government does not rest upon civil administration or physical coercion alone, but upon a combination of the two. The need is to make civil rather than military institutions foremost in the politics of the Province.

## Alternative Ways of Coping

The immediate task of Ulster politicians is not to create consensus where none exists, but to create institutions of civil government that can work without full consensus. In the words of William Whitelaw, former Northern Ireland secretary, the object is to realize "elements of a solution." Everyone who must share in civil government already lives within Northern Ireland and cannot be excluded from participation in the outcome. Some will give their positive consent, whereas others, for want of anything better or for fear of something worse, will passively comply with the law for the time being at least. Those who will neither support the new regime nor comply with its basic political laws will be rebels. If the constitution makers are to be successful, the rebels must be coerced into unwilling compliance. If government cannot do this, Northern Ireland faces the prospect of years more of continuing disorder.

While the groups that must participate in the immediate resolution of the Province's Troubles are known, there can be no certainty about what will happen next. There are more ways to govern without consensus than to govern with it. This chapter reviews the possible alternative outcomes of the current unsettled state of Northern Ireland. Some of the alternatives correspond to the intentions of parties in the 1975 Convention. Others would be the unintentional consequences of decisions and nondecisions arising from the Convention. There is also the possibility that groups outside the Convention might impose a settlement out of the barrel of a gun. The multiplicity of alternatives and the radical differences between them mean that the odds are against predicting precisely what will happen next. Anyone who has studied Ulster politics for long is ready for surprises, even if they take the form of the reappearance of features of a forgotten, irrelevant, or unwanted past. Nevertheless, historical and logical limits make it possible to set out comprehensively the possible alternatives.

The alternative forms of immediately practicable governance for Northern Ireland can be grouped under five broad headings—self-government within the United Kingdom, direct rule from London, independence, unification with Southern Ireland, and destruction. There are a larger number of specific scenarios. While only one form of government can be tried at a time, more than one alternative can be attempted in the course of the next five years. Before deciding what form of government he would most want to promote or to avoid, a prudent Ulsterman will wish to consider the implications of choice. The first question to ask is, *who* is to govern? This concerns not only party politics, but also constitutional and extraconstitutional military forces. Second, *how* is the Province to be governed? This is a problem of adapting or creating political institutions. The third question is, *by what means* is this form of government to come about? There is little point in contemplating an outcome if there is no conceivable way to get there from here. The fourth question—*what consequences* would this regime have for Ulster people?—cannot be answered with scientific precision. Yet consequences, though uncertain, are nonetheless important and some hypothetical outcomes are much more attractive—or much less unpalatable—than others.

## Self-Government within the United Kingdom

While there is an apparent paradox in speaking of self-government for Northern Ireland within the United Kingdom, both Ulstermen and British politicians understand and appreciate the potential advantages of this arrangement. On the one hand, it would leave Ulstermen free to deal with what concerns them most—local problems, discretionary decisions about how public monies are to be spent, and maintaining their own law and order. It would also promise a continuing and substantial flow of cash subsidies from the British Treasury, granted on the redistributive principle of taxation according to ability to pay and expenditure according to evidence of need. The advantages to Britain would be less. Historically, there was military value in having Northern Ireland protect the western approaches of the transatlantic sea link between Britain and North America. Today, the British interest is negative: to prevent the creation of an unfriendly or anarchic state or an ally of an antagonistic power, like Cuba vis-à-vis the United States, close to the heartland of Great Britain. Self-government for the Province would enable Britain to shed de facto responsibility for internal events while retaining nominal de jure sovereignty important in international affairs.

The chief obstacle to self-government is not posed by Britain, but rather by the parties to disputes within the Province, which seem unable to come to terms with each other. As long as power is in British hands, any side can appeal to the British government to support its cause. Under self-government, all would have to appeal to a Northern Ireland electorate and to a Northern Ireland constitution.

**Rule by a Loyalist Majority.** If Northern Ireland were governed like other parts of the United Kingdom, there would be no question about who should govern the Province. Power would be vested in the party or coalition of parties that won the majority of seats in the appropriate Parliament or Assembly. There is no doubt that the candidates of the UUUC won a majority of votes in the three elections held in the Province in 1974–75 (see Table 6). They did so with a larger share of the popular vote than Harold Wilson won in the 1974 British elections, Sir Winston Churchill in 1951, Richard Nixon in the 1968 U.S. presidential contest, or John F. Kennedy in 1960. However, the Troubles make clear that Northern Ireland is, unfortunately, not exactly like other parts of the United Kingdom. The Loyalists wish to return to a British system, that is, government by a cabinet chosen from the ranks of a parliamentary majority, whatever political party or coalition of parties that elected majority represents. This is the form of government that operated for fifty years at Stormont until Westminster suspended it in 1972.

Loyalists accept that some differences' exist between Northern Ireland and other parts of the United Kingdom. The UUUC convention manifesto stated a readiness to vary institutions slightly from the basic Westminster model of government, while emphasizing that "the traditional British democratic parliamentary system is essentially the right one."[1] In view of the ineffectual nature of backbench committees in the British House of Commons, it would not be difficult for Loyalists to offer the Stormont minority parties more power than their British counterparts have. The chief variation proposed in the manifesto is the establishment of all-party committees of backbench M.P.s giving minority parties opportunities to comment on legislation and scrutinize administration. In addition, the UUUC manifesto proposed a bill of rights to provide guarantees for individual members of the minority and to entrench the position of a devolved Northern Ireland Parliament vis-à-vis Westminster.

One argument that Loyalists can advance for the revival of parliamentary government is that it is not only what most Ulstermen want, but also what they are prepared to operate. The creation of a new constitution along Loyalist lines would require endorsement by the British government through an act of the Westminster Parliament. The fact that the Loyalists want to govern the Province is an attraction to any British cabinet anxious to disengage from this most troublesome part of the United Kingdom. Yet the British government in its 1974 Convention White Paper emphasized power sharing and an Irish dimension, as well as acceptance by the British Parliament. In practical political terms, the third condition comes first. Once a British government had decided that it wished to disengage from Northern Ireland by transferring power back to a majority that is eager to have it, the White Paper statement could be subjected to a very wide variety of interpretations. Backbench committees could be construed as power sharing and negotiations with Dublin about repressing the IRA as an Irish dimension. Whether a British government is ready to make this about-face would depend upon the extent of Westminster's weariness of continually sinking men, money, and authority into Northern Ireland, the extent of IRA-inspired violence in England, and possible pressures from a Conservative opposition to back a "British" rather than a "Republican" cause.

The immediate consequence of returning self-government to Northern Ireland on the basis of simple majority rule would be to arouse SDLP fears of its long-term exclusion from power. An IRA campaign might lead the SDLP to see parliamentary opposition as a lesser evil than withdrawal, which would make extraparliamentary

---

[1] *United Ulster Unionist Election Manifesto* (Belfast: Century Services, 1975).

Republicans the chief group articulating Catholic grievances. Alternatively, the SDLP might refuse to cooperate in a British-style parliamentary government, on the ground that generations of exclusion from office had earned its supporters reparation in some form. If control of the security forces were transferred to a Protestant majority at Stormont, activities by Protestant paramilitary groups would presumably be reduced, *provided that* the new regime dealt effectively with the IRA. The one way in which this could be done nonviolently would be through a balance of terror, with IRA forces restrained by fear within the Catholic community of a Protestant backlash and the Protestants restrained by a desire for constitutional rule without violence. If such a risky balance were not achieved, violence could easily erupt from either side. If the scale of violence were no greater than it has been under British protection, Loyalists could claim that the consequences of self-government were satisfactory. But if violence approached a holocaust, the British government would be an accessory before the fact to wholesale slaughter.

**Rule by a Broad Unionist Coalition.** The Loyalist UUUC, the Unionist party of Northern Ireland, and the Alliance party together, representing upwards of 75 percent of the Northern Ireland electorate, could command from two-thirds to four-fifths of the seats in any elected Northern Ireland Assembly. Together, they would constitute a broad coalition that would include every party but the SDLP. (The presence or absence of one Northern Ireland Labour party representative would be of slight significance.) While the Alliance party does not represent the bulk of Catholic voters, it draws a larger proportion of Catholic votes than do Republican Club candidates. By virtue of winning Catholic votes, it is also more sensitive to Catholic opinion than exclusively Protestant-based parties, such as the Loyalists and the UPNI.

A Convention report or a cabinet endorsed by the sixty-one votes of such a broad coalition would not necessarily differ greatly in content from Loyalist recommendations for majority-rule government. It would, however, differ importantly in its political support. The British government would find it difficult to dismiss a government favored by three-quarters of the Province, because this would appear to give the SDLP an absolute veto upon the future government of the Province. The presence of Alliance party Catholics supporting a broad coalition could make majority-rule institutions more acceptable in Britain by indicating that Loyalists use political (that is, anti-Irish) rather than religious (that is, anti-Catholic) criteria in determining their policies. This assumes that the Alliance party would retain its Catholic support after joining a broad coalition.

The chief political consequence of a broad coalition would be the isolation of the SDLP. Conceivably, this might facilitate bargaining across sectarian lines, by weakening the SDLP's demands and encouraging the majority to make concessions from strength, such as the appointment of SDLP men to important nonministerial positions in organizations like the Northern Ireland Housing Executive. But the opposite is also possible: the SDLP might regard its isolation as evidence that Catholic representatives are excluded from power in Northern Ireland, and advocate instead a solution in a thirty-two-county rather than a six-county state.

Power sharing, as the term is currently used in Northern Ireland, means participation in government by the party representing a majority of Catholics, the SDLP, and by parties representing a majority of Protestants. It goes beyond the simple formulae of informal power sharing found within any political organization. It seeks to institutionalize government by a concurring majority composed of two distinct groups, a majority of Protestants and a majority of Catholics. Power-sharing government starts by agreement about who should govern. It also implies a joint and presumptively effective Protestant-Catholic security arrangement that would suppress, by all measures necessary, Republican or Protestant-inspired violence. The power-sharing principle does not, however, specify how institutions of government are to work or by what means a power-sharing government is to come about.

**Power Sharing within a Parliamentary Framework.** Power sharing would most readily come about by electoral swings, or splits and coalitions agreed between parties. Such political deals or electoral movements cannot be written into a constitution. Power sharing could only be institutionalized in a parliamentary-style constitution by such novel requirements as: (1) stipulating that a government could only be formed with the consent of five-sixths of the representative assembly (a "more than majority" rule entrenching a Catholic party's veto); (2) specifying that Catholics should vote on a separate electoral role or qualify for ministerial posts by virtue of their religion (the SDLP, as a nonsectarian party, albeit one representing Catholic voters, would not advocate this); (3) offering posts in government to any party that signified that it was prepared to share power in government (a device that might lead the Loyalists to refuse office, thereby creating an executive which could be defeated on every vote in Parliament); or

(4) requiring any cabinet to receive, before its formation, the endorsement of the British cabinet (a rule that would derogate from self-government and threaten to disrupt parties by creating opposing pressures from London and from Ulster voters).

*Electoral swings.* An SDLP-UPNI-Alliance coalition could command a majority of seats in a Northern Ireland Assembly *if* a small proportion of Ulstermen swung their votes at a subsequent general election. In 1975, the UUUC had eight seats more than it needed to entrench its power in the Convention. The Loyalists won fourteen of their seats without attaining quotas. Such seats are potentially vulnerable to loss in another electoral contest, especially the five seats the Loyalists won by less than 1,000 votes and the three won by less than 2,000 votes. Given that the Loyalists must take about three-quarters of the Protestant vote to have a majority within the Province as a whole, their majority position at Stormont cannot be regarded as permanent under the present system of proportional representation.[2] Under a British- or American-style electoral system, on the other hand, Loyalists would be able to count on a permanent majority at Stormont.

If the Loyalists formed a simple-majority government, they might lose their majority for the reasons that make government unpopular, sooner or later, in almost every other country in the Western world—economic failures, ministerial scandals, or a diffuse popular belief that it is time for a change. Such a loss of power through electoral swings could eventuate *only after* the Loyalists had held office on their own for a substantial period of time. This is not something that their competitors, particularly the SDLP, would regard as acceptable or desirable.

*Party splits.* As its name implies, the United Ulster Unionist Council is a coalition of three political parties, each of which has distinctive features. While some members speak of amalgamating the three groups, others speculate about the possibility of splintering the coalition. The UUUC could lose up to seven members from its Convention strength and still have a majority. If it lost eight to fourteen members (if, for example, one of its three parties broke away), the UUUC could retain a majority by adding Alliance, UPNI, and the one NILP man to its ranks. Another way to look at the same arithmetic

---

[2] The Loyalists could, of course, increase their representation in a subsequent Ulster election. The most likely gains would be three seats now held by UPNI members.

is to say that an SDLP-Alliance-UPNI coalition would need to split off nine or ten UUUC seats in order to constitute a majority.

The history of party politics in any country, Northern Ireland not excepted, is a history of intraparty disagreements, faction fights, potential splits and breakaway movements. The causes of such disruptions are multiple: ideology, personality, regional and age differences. Yet in the winner-take-all parliamentary system there is always one incentive for party unity: the promise of taking all the seats in the cabinet by maintaining discipline in Parliament, however divided the party may be elsewhere. This motive was sufficient to hold the Unionists together for fifty years—and the Loyalists have found in the Convention election that it offered immediate advantages to them as well. Moreover, the disastrous electoral fate of those who in the past have diverged from the mainstream of Unionism or Loyalism to espouse collaboration with Catholics, within or outside Parliament, is a major disincentive to a formal split. Notwithstanding the risk, William Craig threatened to split the UUUC in the Convention in September 1975, when he proposed negotiating a voluntary coalition with the SDLP. Only a subsequent general election could demonstrate whether such a policy could remove sufficient votes from the hard-line Loyalists favoring majority rule to cost them their majority or, even more important, whether it could secure a majority of Protestant votes for a power-sharing-type policy.

*Coalition government.* There would need to be complex negotiations before either the SDLP or Loyalists group would enter into a voluntary coalition agreement. The SDLP would need some kind of informal guarantee that it would not become a prisoner of a larger Loyalist bloc within a coalition. The Loyalists would want evidence that the SDLP were not Republicans, anathema to Protestant voters, but rather Catholic Ulstermen committed to governing Northern Ireland from within Northern Ireland, rather than at the dictates of London, Dublin, or any other power. The SDLP's position is ambivalent, for while it rejects Irish unity through force and accepts de facto government from within the Province, its members nonetheless endorse a long-term aspiration for Irish unity by consent.

The most immediate and dramatic offer that the SDLP could make would be to ask the Republic of Ireland to repudiate its claim to Northern Ireland under Articles 2 and 3 of the Republic of Ireland's current constitution. The purpose of such action would be to establish publicly and unambiguously that the SDLP is not a Republican party as that term is used by Protestants. The SDLP could gain real and tangible power in Ulster in exchange for sacrificing symbolic and intangible advantages of the distant future. The repeal of Articles 2 and 3 would need to be approved by an Irish electorate in a referendum. It could be justified in Southern Ireland as merely a "form of words," leaving unaltered a long-term aspiration to unification by consent.[3] If armed Republican opposition materialized and repeal carried in a referendum, the victory of those opposed to using force to change the border between Northern Ireland and the Republic would then need to be sealed in blood.

**Power Sharing by a Nonparliamentary Representative Government.** Nonparliamentary representative government in which power is shared is practicable, as the United States of America makes evident and as the institutions of French republics intermittently emphasize. Parliamentary government is equated with democracy in Northern Ireland because it is familiar, by imitation of London and by observation of the Irish Dail. Yet parliamentary government is inconsistent with the principle of power sharing used in Northern Ireland, because parliamentary government presupposes power sharing by rotation in office. When elections are held on the constitutional issue, one side always wins a majority and, under the rules, claims all the seats in the cabinet. The minority is unable to restrain a majority government by parliamentary means. Catholic representatives had half a century to learn this under Stormont. The Loyalists found this out when they were in opposition to the power-sharing Executive for five months in 1974; the Executive was broken by an extraparliamentary general strike. A variety of representative but nonparliamentary forms of government can be identified.

*Government by executive committees.* Local government in England does not operate through a cabinet system, but rather through a popularly elected council constituting a set of committees responsible for education, housing, and other functions of local authorities. Each committee normally draws members in proportion to party strength in the local council. Committee members are supposed to be consulted about major policy decisions prior to their announcement and are in contact with senior full-time civil servants carrying out the work for which their committees are responsible. The chairman of the committee may or may not be drawn from the largest party

---

[3] A subsidiary calculation would be the effect of such a referendum upon the fortunes of the party in office in Dublin at the time. For example, a Fine Gael/Labour coalition government might calculate that a successful repeal referendum would split Fianna Fail or drive it closer to the electorally unpopular Republicans, thus increasing support for the parties in power.

in the council, depending upon local practices. In effect the cabinet is abolished, and committee chairmen are the most important members of the elected council.

In practice, English local government usually does not involve power sharing, at least in the larger cities where party politics is fully developed. The party that wins the most seats in the local election takes all the committee chairmanships. It constitutes a coordinating group, equivalent to a cabinet, to which chairmen of committees are appointed. Party discipline prevents the minority party—Conservative in the major cities and Labour in suburban and rural areas—from carrying out its distinctive policies. In places where one-party dominance has long been the rule (for example, in mining areas controlled by local Labour parties or in farming areas controlled by Conservatives) there are few or no signs of power sharing.

*A separately elected executive.* The American system of government institutionalizes power sharing by vesting executive power in a President elected by a nationwide constituency very different from the districts electing individual congressmen. In consequence, the White House and Congress can be, and often are, in the hands of opposing parties. Even when they are in the same hands, loyalty to different constituencies creates many restraints upon unilateral action. A presidential executive would not create power sharing in Northern Ireland, quite apart from the personal jealousies it would excite among politicians, because it would always be won by a Protestant if the Loyalists maintained any degree of unity.

Power sharing could also be realized through the creation of a popularly elected plural executive. An eight-man executive elected by proportional representation would result in a cabinet of five Loyalists, two SDLP members, and one Alliance member, judging by the Convention election results. The election of such figures by a Province-wide ballot would tend to undermine the localism that is very prominent in Ulster politics and would invest those so elected with considerable authority within their parties. Specific ministerial offices could be chosen in order among the parties. The Loyalists, choosing first, might take finance, the SDLP commerce, Alliance law reform, and so on. Junior ministers could be appointed by the parties in proportion to their strength in the Assembly—but from outside Assembly ranks. Security might best be managed by a separate security authority, its members elected by the parties in the Assembly in proportion to their strength there. These arrangements would separate "normal" (that is, socioeconomic) issues from "real" (that is, security) issues—while making each accountable through representative elections. Insofar as discretionary decisions within the hands of an individual cabinet minister are important, these would be divided out among different parties. Insofar as legislation is important, this would be controlled by the party or parties with a majority in the Assembly. Each party would require a strong man to lead its Assembly team. The task of governing would be to combine party loyalties and departmental patronage in order to gain for each minister sufficient backing from those whose interests were affected by his department. This would be American-style politics (for which Ulstermen have a ready instinctive understanding), rather than the non-power-sharing politics of Westminster.

*Federalism.* The federal system seeks to share power by dividing it on a geographical basis. In a federal structure, many powers that in Britain are lodged in Parliament are assigned to regional authorities. Such a structure of government presupposes a large element of political agreement within each region as well as social differences between the various regions into which a state is divided. This is the essence of the Swiss system of cantonal government. A federal solution would not work in Northern Ireland because an admixture of Protestants and Catholics is found throughout the Province. The number of regions controlled by the Catholic minority would, under almost any conceivable boundaries, be few; the majority of the Catholics would find themselves in cantons in which the bulk of the electorate was Protestant. In other words, federalism would reproduce rather than resolve the problems presented by majority-rule government at Stormont.

*Vesting power in boards and corporations outside the structure of cabinet government.* Every modern government, including that of Great Britain, has created a plethora of semiautonomous agencies and boards that vest government power in the hands of appointed officials who are the immediate controllers of nationalized industries, central banks, regulatory commissions, development agencies such as the Tennessee Valley Authority, and so on. Forty-six such bodies already exist in Northern Ireland, ranging in importance from the Housing Executive to the Seed Potato Marketing Board. The reorganization of local government increased rather than diminished the importance of appointive bodies. Whatever professors of public administration may think of such agencies, there are good political reasons for fragmenting power in this way—insofar as one wishes to encourage power sharing. When powers are divided in the execution of government policy, more than one party may share in their exercise. This already happens in education, where the Catholic hierarchy runs Catholic schools—though with less money than is provided to the state schools and with less control by popularly elected officials. Under the old Stormont regime, appointive offices were not allotted proportionately among communities. A tabulation of the religion of appointees to nine major boards in the sixth year of Terence O'Neill's period as prime minister found 115 Protestants and 16 Catholics. Among judicial and legal appointees, there were 68 Protestants and 6 Catholics.[4]

The direction of a specified number of major government boards could be determined by party choice and in proportion to party strength in the Assembly. This would give each party an outlet for constructive effort. The Assembly would retain control of finance through the annual budget, and the cabinet would have broad responsibilities for legislation and for recommending the budget. The Assembly could, for example, check the Housing Executive by denyings funds—but it would be likely to do so only if it did not make itself unpopular among Ulstermen who wished the government to spend more money on housing.

## Direct Rule from London

Each of the foregoing forms of self-government could be denounced as impractical, unacceptable, or both by one or more significant political parties within the Province. If all of these alternatives were to be rejected, the default position for governing Ulster is direct rule from London.

**Continuing Direct Rule.** This is the system that has been employed in Northern Ireland since April 1972, except for the five months of the power-sharing Executive. Within the British cabinet, the secretary of state for Northern Ireland is formally responsible for administering the powers vested in the Northern Ireland Executive and in the British government, and the secretary of state for defense is responsible for the security operations of the British military. Any legislation must be passed by the British Parliament, and the Northern Ireland secretary is answerable for his actions to 635 United Kingdom M.P.s, of whom 12 are from Ulster. The arrangement has worked in a straightforward bureaucratic fashion in handling "normal" (that is, social and economic) issues. The Northern Ireland Civil Service, a permanent, separately recruited body, provides the manpower, exper-

---

[4] See Harbinson, *Ulster Unionist Party*, p. 118 f.

tise, and local knowledge to maintain the everyday services of the modern welfare state; it advises the Northern Ireland Office officials and British ministers.

Direct rule has left the British army and other security officers free to deal with "real" (that is, security) problems unhindered by the need to be responsible to any elected Northern Ireland assembly. London assumes that only an outsider can govern the Province fairly. The secretary of state for Northern Ireland can give as little or as much attention as he wishes to the views of Ulster representatives. Merlyn Rees created ill will among local politicians by his unreadiness to discuss their constituents' problems, while concurrently his officials were accessible to paramilitary and even illegal organizations. Powerless because their assembly is in suspense, those elected to the Northern Ireland Convention are nonetheless the legitimate representatives of people in the Province.

One important political consequence of direct rule is that elected representatives in Ulster are not committed to supporting the government, because none holds office under it nor does the secretary of state belong to the same party as any M.P.s from Northern Ireland. Since 1974, none of the twelve Ulster M.P.s at Westminster has wished to affiliate himself with a British party; thus, none has any claim to be given office by the governing party of the day, because British parliamentary conventions are based upon adversary politics rather than power sharing. No Ulster politician need defend the decisions of the secretary of state, however popular they may be in Britain. From a Northern Ireland perspective, direct rule by a Westminster-based secretary has the appearance of colonial rule by a governor-general—indeed, by a colonial ruler who replaces a popularly elected local government.

The existing institutions of direct rule are interim arrangements. The institutions of local government in Northern Ireland, for example, presuppose the existence of a powerful, locally controlled representative assembly at Stormont. Moreover, both Conservative and Labour governments have regarded direct rule as temporary; it operates by annually renewable legislation while Parliament seeks to transfer the powers of government back to the Province. Politically, the arrangements are unstable, because sooner or later they tend to unite *all* Northern Ireland politicians against rule by a London government that is not accountable to them. In turn, this offers the initiative to paramilitary groups in Ulster to use violence to resolve disagreements.

**Integration with Great Britain.** When the British government displays an unwillingness to trust Ulstermen with substantial self-government, some Loyalists retort: treat Northern Ireland as if it were like any other piece of British soil. The object of this request is to integrate the Province into Britain in such a way that it could no more fall under government from Dublin than might Birmingham, Manchester, or Leeds. Legislation and political responsibility could rest at Westminster, and the local government of Northern Ireland could be taken over by institutions comparable to the major institutions of local government elsewhere in Britain. Full integration would mean the allocation of the same proportion of Westminster M.P.s to Northern Ireland as the proportions Scotland and Wales enjoy, an increase from twelve to about twenty seats. It would also mean a seat in the British cabinet for an Ulster secretary, preferably an Ulsterman, since the Scottish and Welsh secretaries are expected to come from their parts of the United Kingdom. Ulstermen who favor integration accept the prospect of an alternation in government by Labour and Conservatives as a bulwark against government by such Dublin-based parties as Fianna Fail and Fine Gael. Those who oppose integration do so because, inter alia, it would remove Stormont as a bulwark against London's selling out the Province to Dublin.

The integration of Northern Ireland could come about if the British Parliament wished to insist upon the Britishness of Ulster, as its nineteenth-century predecessors insisted upon the crown's claim to the whole of Ireland. In the nineteenth century, religion rather than geography tended to influence relations between Englishmen and Irishmen. Protestants were accepted as British and Catholics were regarded as an inferior caste or race. Today, geography rather than religion is crucial. The bloody Troubles since 1969 have only emphasized the alienness of Ulster to Englishmen. Both BBC announcers and English civil servants often refer to the people of Ulster as Irishmen, even though many Ulstermen insist that they are British. British politicians have no wish to end the institutional anomalies and uncertainties arising from direct rule by integrating what is now often regarded as an alien part of the United Kingdom. Just as Ulstermen might veto British decisions about their part of the United Kingdom, so British M.P.s could veto Northern Ireland's intruding further into Great Britain. Increased Westminster responsibilities in Ulster are formally opposed on the grounds that the problems there are atypical and unsuitable for Westminster's governance. Extra seats for Northern Ireland M.P.s would also make it more difficult for either the Labour or the Conservative party to win a majority of seats at

Westminster. Moreover, the trend within Great Britain is toward devolution to elected assemblies in Edinburgh and Cardiff. Some Ulstermen who appreciate this argue, "Give us integration *and* devolved institutions on a parity with Scotland and Wales."

## An Independent Northern Ireland

The idea of an independent Northern Ireland state is discussed from time to time as a way to resolve the conflicts within Ulster by negating a central desire of each community. Protestants would give up their link with Britain and Catholics their aspiration for unity with the Republic. Insofar as such symbols are important (and one should never underestimate their significance in Northern Ireland), two causes of the conflict would be removed. One effect of British policies since 1969 has been to encourage a significant number of Ulster Protestants to think in terms of independence (on the model of Canada or New Zealand) as offering the best protection of their Britishness. There would be no difficulty, in principle or in international law, in the creation of an independent Northern Ireland state. Since 1945, the British government has given independence to dozens of former territories, many less populous and with fewer resources than Northern Ireland. The fate of many such territories might give Ulstermen pause before demanding independence—but that is not the worry of Great Britain.

### A Unilateral Declaration of Independence by a Group of Loyalists.
A unilateral declaration by Loyalists is the most frequently discussed means by which independence might be achieved. In the event of an attempt by a British government to force Ulster into the Republic of Ireland, many Ulster Loyalists are ready to resist by all means at hand. Undoubtedly, there are within Northern Ireland sufficient Protestants to form a provisional government and thousands of armed men who might prefer independence to being sold to the South by Britain. To initiate a unilateral declaration of independence would, however, be another matter. The progenitors of such a move would have to allow for two very different contingencies. On the one hand, the British army might fight in defense of its established positions. That, plus likely Republican resistance, would intensify warfare within the Province rather than end it. The other is that the British army might accept a coup and withdraw, leaving a state that would be isolated outside the European Economic Community (EEC), with few capital

resources and the major internal security problem presented by the Republicans.

**Negotiated Independence.** A British government confronted with a demand from Ulster Loyalists for the return of self-government to Northern Ireland might decide to cut its losses by counterproposing to negotiate independence. Such a situation could come about, say, if the British government voted down the Convention's report in the British House of Commons and submitted counterproposals to the Ulster people through a referendum. If Westminster's plans were rejected because the Loyalists campaigned against them, at this impasse Britain might offer to negotiate independence. It could provide, for instance, seven-year terminal transitional economic grants and offer to sponsor Ulster's membership in the EEC, subject, of course, to a Dublin veto. It might also negotiate a military treaty giving Britain the right to send troops to Northern Ireland in case of threats to joint security. It would then be up to events to show whether Britain would regard internal violence in Ulster as requiring the dispatch of British troops, or whether this would happen only in the event of actions by governments outside the British Isles.

The consequences of an independent Northern Ireland present substantial risks for both Protestants and Catholics. British subsidies that now come to the Province as of right, as one of the poorer and therefore needier parts of the United Kingdom, would be lost. (The discovery of oil off Northern Ireland's shores would end this concern—but the oil being exploited off the shores of Scotland has not been close to Northern Ireland's coastline.) While Republicans might welcome an independent Northern Ireland as the first stage in the creation of new political institutions throughout the island, many Catholics in Ulster would regard being governed by a Protestant majority in an independent state as even riskier than being governed under the old Stormont regime.

### Unification with Southern Ireland

For centuries, the thirty-two counties of Ireland were governed as one country under the English crown. In the debates about home rule in the late nineteenth century, both Protestants and Catholics assumed that a single government would control Ireland—though they disputed whether Dublin or London should be the locus of sovereignty. The Republican uprising of 1916 led to the partition of Ireland, after the conflicting armed forces had each proved dominant in part of the island's territory. Separate governments were established in Dublin and Belfast, one under the crown, the other as a Republic. The two parts might come together again in any of three very different relationships.

**A Federal Ireland.** The institutions of federalism are well understood throughout the English-speaking world. In the Irish case, federalism might involve (1) two separate governments along existing divisions, (2) the return to a "four-provinces" Ireland, Ulster plus the three historic Southern regions of Leinster, Munster, and Connacht, or (3) three provinces, with the Gaelic-speaking rural West given substantial autonomy vis-à-vis the East and the North. The capital need not be located in Dublin; Athlone in the Republic or the cathedral town of Armagh in Ulster might be equally suitable as the capital of a federal government. The limited powers of the federal government would have to include provision for finance, foreign affairs, and internal order; otherwise it would not be a government. Northern Catholics and Southern Irishmen advocate a federal Ireland because they see it as a Republican institution, drawing Northern Ireland out of the United Kingdom rather than leading the South back to institutions it rejected after more than 700 years of British overlordship. A federal Ireland remains merely a theoretical possibility, because Ulster Protestants refuse to countenance the idea—except on the condition that the South rejoin the United Kingdom.

**British-Irish Condominium Rule.** Logically, if both Britain and the Republic claim jurisdiction over Ulster, both might be expected to share in ruling it. This idea was embodied in the 1972 SDLP proposal, *Towards a New Ireland*, recommended as an interim measure pending Irish unity on terms acceptable throughout Ireland. To administer joint sovereignty, the SDLP proposed the appointment of two commissioners, one from each country, to approve all legislation, to oversee the workings of an elected Executive, and to appoint a constitutional court. Such a condominium would rest upon authority external to the Province and, conversely, would run the risk of inadequate support within the Province. Ulster Protestants have always rejected any interference by Dublin in Ulster affairs—and would redouble their resistance if a condominium were urged as a transition to Irish unity.

**The Transfer of Northern Ireland to the Republic of Ireland.** In international law, a transfer would appear simple, for any sovereign state has the power to cede part of its territory. The measure, more-over, could be given a gloss of democratic authority by a plebiscite in which a majority of citizens in the United Kingdom and in the Republic voted for such a transfer of territory. In practical political terms, such a transfer could not be peacefully consummated. In the first instance, the Republic of Ireland would hesitate to incorporate 1 million Protestants without their consent into a new state with 3 million Catholics. It would transfer the problem of governing without consensus from Belfast to Dublin, inviting the creation of an armed Protestant resistance more formidable than that which Ulster Republicans have heretofore offered Stormont rule. The intensity of Protestant resistance to Dublin rule would be compounded by the belief that Britain had violated its repeated pledge that Northern Ireland would not be ceded to the Republic without the consent of its people, whether given by a majority of an elected assembly or by a plebiscite in Northern Ireland. (The 1973 referendum on the border issue produced a 98.9 percent vote in favor of remaining within the United Kingdom, on a turnout of 58.7 percent.) In such circum-stances, Protestant paramilitary groups would almost certainly re-taliate by a massive bombing campaign in Dublin intended to exceed the worst already suffered in Belfast. The desire to avoid unifying Ireland through violence makes the government of the relatively peaceful twenty-six-county Republic avoid a policy of unity at any price.

At no time during the current Troubles has the Dublin govern-ment actively sought the unification of the thirty-two counties. To do so would be to run two risks: first, that the Irish Republican movement would seize the initiative from government forces, since it is the IRA that has for decades been campaigning actively for Irish unity, and second, that several hundred thousand Catholics living in predominantly Protestant parts of Northern Ireland would be threat-ened with retaliatory attacks by their Protestant neighbors. Even so, the present Fine Gael foreign secretary, Garrett FitzGerald, in a book published in 1972, could expand in detail upon the shape of a new and united Ireland.[5] His opposite number in the traditionally more Republican Fianna Fail party, Michael O'Kennedy, simultaneously rejects violence and "the right of a majority within Northern Ireland to determine freely the character of the relationship of Northern Ireland with our state." [6] While Ulster Protestants note the resurgence

---

[5] Garrett FitzGerald, *Towards a New Ireland* (London: Charles Knight, 1972), Chapter 10.
[6] "O'Kennedy Rejects Minister's N. I. View," *Irish Times*, 29 September 1975.

of those long-term aspirations for Irish unification, Ulster Catholics note complaints from the Irish minister of defense about the burden of policing the border and his insistence that the Republic of Ireland's limited defense force would never be used in Northern Ireland, regardless of the situation prevailing there.[7] This policy leaves Britain with the responsibility for stopping disorder in Northern Ireland should things get out of hand there. It leaves Ulster Catholics to look to local Republican sources for self-defense, rather than to the official forces of the Irish Republic.

## The Destruction of Northern Ireland

In fits of exasperation, politicians who do not belong to Northern Ireland are tempted to mutter: "The only thing to do with the place is to get rid of it." The more or less well-intentioned people who speak thus are not prescribing a final solution in the manner of Hitler's attempt to exterminate European Jewry. Nonetheless, those who so casually speak of the disruption of another people's land might remember the Second World War slogan, "Loose Talk Costs Lives." Ulstermen speak very cautiously and warily about anything that might disrupt the world as they know it.

Destruction of the Northern Ireland that its people know could arise from the movement of international boundaries (that is, repartition) and/or the forced movement of people across international boundaries. Few politicians would actively recommend the destruction of Northern Ireland. Many fear that it might come about by default, following the failure of other efforts at settlement, and despair of finding any terms on which Ulstermen might live peacefully together. Those with a historical sense recall that the Troubles of half a century ago were not resolved by peaceful negotiation, but rather by partition of a nine-county Ulster along lines that the Protestants considered militarily defensible in circumstances of internal war.

**Repartition by Local Option Ballot.** In the 1973 border referendum, the British government refused to allow votes to be counted by local government units within the Province, because this would have shown that there are areas, particularly near the border, where a majority of residents wish to unite with the Republic. It would also have highlighted areas in the East of the Province, including Belfast, where the

---

[7] "Donnegan's Army," *Hibernia* (Dublin), 19 September 1975.

desire for union with Britain is very strong. The breakdown of constitutional negotiations could again bring up the idea of repartitioning Ulster.

The basic principle of a local option poll is that the majority in an area decides the fate of everybody living there—in this case whether all would be assigned to the Republic of Ireland or to Northern Ireland. A local option referendum would differ from the 1973 poll in that the areas within which votes were counted would be smaller than the whole six counties. This would allow areas where Republicans are in a local majority to opt out of Northern Ireland, without breaching the basic principle of majority rule. Prior to the reorganization of local government in 1973, the six counties of the Province were divided into sixty-seven administrative areas; today, they consist of twenty-six district councils. The following figures are derived from 1971 census data for the boundaries of the sixty-seven old local government areas. Dividing the Province into a larger number of areas increases the statistical probability that the Catholic minority will, at some points, constitute a majority.[8]

If voting were strictly along religious lines, then, according to 1971 census figures, fourteen predominantly rural areas would opt to join the Republic. These are the areas where Catholics are in an absolute majority, and they include parts of each of the six counties of Northern Ireland. In addition, another four areas might go Republican, inasmuch as at least 45 percent of the population report themselves as Catholics, and of those who refused to state their religion a sufficient number could be Catholic to give the Republic a majority.

Most of the administrative areas with an absolute majority of Catholics are on the border or contiguous to Catholic areas on the border. There are also four islands of Catholics surrounded by unambiguously Protestant areas. They are very small: the largest, Armagh town, had a population of 11,663 in 1971. The border areas where Catholics predominate are generally agricultural districts where the land is poor, or the small market towns serving them. The one commercial and industrial center, the city of Londonderry, has been a depressed area for half a century. Catholics would argue that this is because the 1921 partition isolated Derry from its natural hinterland in Republican Donegal.

Politically, a local option ballot would resolve little. First of all, it would create wrangles about what to do with Catholic or Protestant islands totally surrounded by areas of opposite persuasion. Second,

---

[8] For full details, see Richard Rose and Ian McAllister, "Repartition Not the Solution to Northern Ireland's Problems," *Irish Times*, 16 September 1975.

161

repartition would not eliminate political minorities, but would simply alter their proportions. The maximum transfer of eighteen border areas into the Republic would remove 161,142 Catholics from Northern Ireland. But it would still leave, according to the same census figures, 316,779 Catholics in what was meant to be a British and Protestant state. It would only reduce the size of the Catholic minority from 34.7 percent to 28.1 percent of the population. Moreover, it would "depatriate" 89,807 Protestants into the Republic. In areas west of the River Bann, where the result of any border poll is likely to be close, there would be a strong incentive for the losers to concentrate upon all measures necessary to guarantee them victory next time.[9] Whatever decisions might be negotiated about an overall exchange of population, they would not be unanimously acceptable in every local district.

Repartition is unlikely to come about as a result of peaceful electoral measures—especially in a Province where extralegal armies compete with each other. If the government should adopt the principle that the majority in each area has the right to decide for everyone what nationality the territory will have, the corollary would clearly be that the minority has no rights. The Ulster and Irish governments would not need to take positive measures to remove minorities; paramilitary groups would do it for them. If the pattern of the 1921 partition were repeated, tens of thousands of Protestants who found themselves in the Republic would undoubtedly move into the Protestant part of Ulster. Then, if the pattern of intimidation established in 1969–70 were followed, Catholics would be driven out of their homes to make way for the displaced Protestants from "lost" areas and the latter would have every incentive to lead the action. The larger the number of Catholics who might be transferred to the Republic by a border referendum, the larger the number of Protestants who would also be displaced.

A local option policy would not be a recipe for the peaceful resolution of minority problems, but rather would result in the creation of a refugee problem on the scale of Palestine's—complete with cross-border raids and incidents of international terrorism launched in the name of irredentist groups. Even the aspirations of the Republican movement would not be satisfied by repartition, for the Republican goal is not an all-Catholic twenty-eight and one-half or

---

[9] These figures make no allowance for the fact that in three of the fifteen Belfast urban wards Catholics are in a majority, albeit in a minority in the city, or that Protestants are in a majority in two of the three wards of the City of Londonderry, albeit in a minority in the city as a whole.

twenty-nine-county Ireland, but rather, a thirty-two-county Ireland. For this the Republicans will battle on till eternity.

**Doomsday.** This is the term colloquially used to describe the military destruction of Northern Ireland. After the failure of one of the disputed but recognizable instruments of civil government described here, or after a succession of such failures, civil authority in the Province might lapse, to be replaced by rule by local armed bands and a movement of population on a scale unseen in Europe since the spring of 1945. Doomsday is worth describing, for all its horror, because those who do not wish to think about it should be seeking to prevent its realization in flesh and in blood.

In Doomsday circumstances, Protestant and Catholic paramilitary forces would not clash with each other on carefully segregated battlefields, but rather would fight street by street, visiting parts of Belfast with destruction of life and property as heavy as that of wartime Warsaw and wreaking terror in the countryside comparable to the brutalities of the 1920s—shooting farmers in the field, burning churches, bombing pubs and shops ad infinitum. The eruption of civil war simultaneously in all parts of the Province would find the British army overextended. Today the army lacks sufficient manpower to maintain civil order against simultaneous challenges in all the towns of the Province, not to mention the countryside. It could patrol the streets of Belfast in armored cars and maintain so-called peace lines (actually large metal fences that resemble miniature Berlin walls) at the most obvious flashpoints. But the number of potential flashpoints is greater than the British army's manpower. In military terms Doomsday might be defined as a situation in which the British army was no longer continuously informed about fighting within the Province. At such a time, the Republic of Ireland might find that its armed forces, too, were out of control, with some units, without regard to orders from Dublin, more or less openly breaching international boundaries to offer arms or men to their coreligionists in the North.

Just as big nations live in dread of an atomic incident, so Northern Ireland lives in dread of a Stone Age incident that might trigger a local holocaust. A shoot-out between the British army and local defense groups or some particularly bloody reprisal for a sectarian murder could escalate into Doomsday. So, too, could a well-intentioned but ill-conceived gesture on the part of a British government official—for example, a statement that the transfer of Northern Ireland to the Republic was under consideration or the leak of a plan for repartition unacceptable to the Ulstermen it would require to change homes or loyalties. There are at least three ways by which political groups within Northern Ireland could bring Doomsday about.

*A Protestant-led pogrom.* A pogrom is an organized massacre of a minority group by a majority, for example, the Russian czar's campaign against the Jews, the Nazi genocidal campaign against Jews, or the massive slaughter of Muslims and Hindus in border areas of British India. Pogroms have not been known in Ulster since the seventeenth century. There have been many killings, but none as sweeping or systematic as a massacre. For example, the street fighting in Belfast in August 1969 was disorganized and only seven people— very few, by the standards of subsequent events—died in the "casual" violence there. A pogrom might take the form of Protestant military units' attacking Catholic areas in West Belfast with mortar shells, their invading an isolated Catholic housing estate with armored cars, burning and shooting until all the inhabitants are gone, or their launching deliberate attacks upon buildings crowded with Catholics. Catholics do not dismiss such attacks as inconceivable. They know the ground upon which they stand. To be forewarned is to be forearmed. The street fighting and intimidation that characterized Belfast in August 1969 would not recur in the same form, because Catholics are now well enough organized and armed to prevent Protestants from marching easily through Catholic streets. Just as American, British, and Russian military commanders store nuclear weapons as a deterrent intended to prevent the unthinkable from being realized, so Ulster Catholics keep as safe as possible from British army searches modern weapons equivalent to "a pike in the thatch," just in case no one is there to defend them the next time trouble comes.

*A Republican uprising.* In August 1969, Protestants interpreted the barricading of the Bogside of Londonderry and similar actions in Catholic parts of Belfast as the start of a rebellion. From a Protestant perspective, it would be neither surprising nor unusual for people who sing rebel songs and fly rebel flags actually to rebel. Nor do the Protestants reckon that there is anything wrong with putting down a rebellion. Republicans would share the premise that rebellion is expected, while seeking a different outcome. Confronted with proposals for the government of Northern Ireland that Republicans regarded as totally unacceptable, IRA leaders would have to choose continuing sporadic violence, an indefinite truce, or a rising which, even if militarily unsuccessful in the first instance, might undermine the status quo and sooner or later encourage successful resistance.

This last was the strategy of the small band of Republicans who seized the Dublin post office in the Easter rising of 1916. They died, but their gesture worked. In contemporary circumstances, a Republican rising would probably not take the form of the symbolic seizure of a public building. It might involve some or all of the following: an assassination campaign against politicians, bombings of crowded public places in Ulster and England, sniping operations against British soldiers, and occasional attacks against "military" objectives. The failure of British-led security forces to repress such attacks could escalate violence further, leading Protestant groups to launch a pogrom against the Catholic community in order to drain the loch in which Republicans swim.

*A unilateral British withdrawal from Ulster.* There is more than one way in which Britain might effectively pull out of Ulster. In the preceding instances, it has been assumed that Britain would formally transfer power to some other body. To withdraw unilaterally (as Britain did in Palestine in 1948) is to leave a vacuum. It would be unprecedented for a modern European state to withdraw unilaterally from an integral part of its own territory without regard for the consequences. But to the extent that continued involvement alienates Britain, then Northern Ireland is considered a remote and troublesome colony. Withdrawal could be seen, in effect, as a unilateral declaration of *British* independence from the United Kingdom of Great Britain and Northern Ireland.

In this event, the arbitrament of force would be the only way to decide who rules where. Ulster Catholics would undoubtedly look to the Republic for military aid—whether from the established Dublin government or from IRA sources. Ulster Protestants would probably accept repartition as a realistic military target and do their best to create a secure Protestant enclave by the forced removal of hundreds of thousands of Catholics.

Even Doomsday would resolve little. It would create havoc far worse than anything seen in Ireland in centuries, and those who emerged alive from the struggle would have to start once again to assemble the institutions of everyday life, including the contentious but nonetheless indispensable institutions of government and public order.

### The Way Ahead

Faced with such alternatives, the ordinary Englishman or American is tempted to abandon any desire to understand the politics of Northern Ireland. Often, the governments of Britain and the Republic of

Ireland choose to pretend that the problem of Northern Ireland does not exist. The people of Northern Ireland are not so fortunately placed. They cannot abandon all concern with government—if only for fear of what would follow. A half-century of government by Stormont demonstrates that it is possible to govern without consensus, for a time at least. The success of Republicans and of Protestant groups in destroying two régimes since is a reminder of the vulnerability of governments not based upon full consent.

The problem confronting all politicians concerned with Northern Ireland is how to build and maintain a majority for *any* regime. In a divided society the existence of enemies has at least one reassuring feature: it implies some friends as well. The art of governing is to balance the two. After political authority has been shaken to its foundations through rebellion, the suspension of regimes, terror, and counterterror, there are many choices open to Ulstermen. Logical reasons can be given why each and every one of the foregoing choices is unworkable. Heartfelt reasons can also be given why any or all of them is unacceptable. This is inevitable in a land doomed to government without consensus. To demonstrate that every conceivable alternative is unacceptable, unworkable, or both, however, is not to dispose of the Northern Ireland problem: the absence of civil government and public order.

It would be gratuitous, even impertinent, for anyone who himself does not have to live with the risks they face to tell the people of Northern Ireland how they ought to govern themselves. The way ahead is uncertain, and the difference between success and failure may be fatal. The author of this book cannot prescribe a cure for a disturbance that appears organic. Instead of prescribing what ought to happen, one can only emphasize what must be avoided. It is hoped that the outcome of the current Troubles will not encompass the destruction of a land where people have been hard tried and shown courage in persevering in the face of great adversity.

We do not know how long the killing and destruction, now in its sixth year, will continue. Nor do we know how it will end. Even less do we know who, if anyone, will claim satisfaction from the result. We will have to await the unfolding of events, many with precedents in bloody and contentious periods of the past, and perhaps a few that are unprecedented. When the time comes for the restoration of civil government to Northern Ireland, it may be difficult to say who has won. We will only know that the Troubles have once again ended because of the palpable, even brutal, evidence that someone has lost.

## The Mechanics of Vote Transfers

The procedure for transferring votes and awarding seats under the rules of the single transferable vote proportional representation election system is best understood by example. The Convention election count in West Belfast illustrates most of the procedures that arise. It also makes very clear how Ulster people line up in a constituency that is a traditional "cockpit" of Northern Ireland politics, for it includes both the exclusively Catholic Falls Road and the Protestant Shankill Road.[1]

A total of fifteen candidates contested the six seats, and 35,720 valid votes were cast. In order to be sure to win a seat, a candidate had to secure 5,103 votes, that is, one vote more than one-seventh of the total.

(1) At the first count, two candidates polled more than the needed quota: John Laird, an Official Unionist, won 8,433 votes and Paddy Devlin, an SDLP candidate, 6,267 votes. Laird thus had a surplus of 3,330 and Devlin of 1,164.

(2) At the second count, Laird's surplus of 3,330 was distributed in proportion to the second preferences indicated by all those who had voted for him. This increased the votes of other candidates as follows:

|  | Candi-dates | Transferred Votes | |
|---|---|---|---|
|  |  | Number | Percent |
| Loyalists | 3 | 3,186 | 95.7 |
| SDLP, Republican, Catholic | 7 | 10 | 0.3 |
| Alliance | 1 | 70 | 2.1 |
| Communist party of Ireland | 2 | 1 | 0.0 |
| Not transferred | — | 63 | 1.9· |

[1] West Belfast figures cited from official election results.

Nineteen out of twenty of Laird's supporters transferred within the Loyalist fold and only one in 250 gave a second preference to a Catholic candidate. None of the Loyalists achieved the required quota with Laird's transfers.

(3) At the third count, Devlin's surplus of 1,164 votes was distributed in proportion to the second preferences of his supporters.

| | Candi- dates | Transferred Votes | |
| | | Number | Percent |
|---|---|---|---|
| Loyalists | 3 | 2 | 0.2 |
| SDLP | 3 | 860 | 73.9 |
| Republican | 5 | 37 | 3.2 |
| Independent Catholic | 1 | 81 | 7.0 |
| Alliance | 1 | 132 | 11.3 |
| Not transferred | — | 52 | 4.5 |

The transfers showed that three-quarters of Devlin's voters gave their votes to his SDLP running mates, and another 10.3 percent swung to other candidates within the Catholic or Republican camp. Catholic transfers to the Alliance candidate, Bob Cooper, were larger than those received from Protestant voters in the previous count.

(4) At the fourth count, the returning officer lumped together the 1,509 votes of five candidates who between them held the bottom places, and three Republican and two Communist party of Ireland candidates were eliminated. This had the following effect:

| | Candi- dates | Transferred Votes | |
| | | Number | Percent |
|---|---|---|---|
| Loyalists | 3 | 51 | 3.4 |
| SDLP | 3 | 379 | 25.1 |
| Independent Catholic | 1 | 168 | 11.1 |
| Alliance | 1 | 184 | 12.2 |
| Not transferred | — | 727 | 48.2 |

The high proportion of nontransferable votes in this ballot reflects the relative exclusiveness of the appeal of Republican and Communist candidates.

(5) The first four counts left Tom Conaty, the independent Catholic candidate, with 2,302, an increase of 250 from his initial first-preference total, which had ranked him exactly in the middle, eighth among fifteen candidates. But at the fifth count, Conaty had become the bottom man. Five candidates below him had been eliminated, and two who had collected fewer first preferences—Jean Coul-

ter, an Official Unionist, and Des Gillespie, SDLP—had passed him, their support augmented by transfers from John Laird and Paddy Devlin respectively. Conaty's "one-man" party was in a bad position to attract transfers, for he had no running mate whose first-preference supporters might have swung to Conaty after being eliminated. The fifth count produced the following distribution of Conaty's votes:

| | Candi-dates | Transferred Votes | |
|---|---|---|---|
| | | Number | Percent |
| Loyalists | 3 | 14 | 0.6 |
| SDLP | 3 | 1,454 | 63.2 |
| Alliance | 1 | 662 | 28.8 |
| Not transferred | — | 172 | 7.5 |

While Conaty ran as a Catholic anti-SDLP candidate, nearly two-thirds of his support transferred to the SDLP; more than one-quarter, however, went to the Alliance candidate, a Protestant.

(6) As the number of candidates fell, the minimum number of votes a candidate required to remain in the running increased. At the sixth count, a DUP candidate, Mrs. Edith Goligher, was eliminated; her 2,689 votes placed her last among the seven candidates still in the running.

| | Candi-dates | Transferred Votes | |
|---|---|---|---|
| | | Number | Percent |
| Loyalists | 2 | 2,346 | 87.2 |
| SDLP | 3 | 10 | 0.4 |
| Alliance | 1 | 87 | 3.2 |
| Not transferred | — | 246 | 9.1 |

This round of transfers gave Jean Coulter more than a quota by adding 1,475 votes to her fifth round total of 4,236. Miss Coulter was thus awarded the third seat.

(7) Miss Coulter's surplus of 608 votes above the quota was distributed at the seventh count.

| | Candi-dates | Transferred Votes | |
|---|---|---|---|
| | | Number | Percent |
| Loyalists | 1 | 557 | 91.6 |
| SDLP | 3 | 4 | 0.7 |
| Alliance | 1 | 45 | 7.4 |
| Not transferred | — | 3 | 0.5 |

The bulk of Miss Coulter's surplus was transferred virtually as a bloc to the one remaining Loyalist candidate, Hugh Smyth, an independent backed by the Volunteer Political party and not endorsed by the UUUC.

(8) At the eighth count, there were only five candidates, and three seats remained to be filled. The bottom candidate, Pascal O'Hare of the SDLP, was eliminated and his 3,121 accumulated votes distributed among the four remaining candidates.

| Candidate | Vote—end of 7th count | Transfers | | Vote—end of 8th count |
|---|---|---|---|---|
| | | Number | Percent | |
| Smyth, Independent Loyalist | 4,685 | +9 | 0.3 | 4,694* |
| Cooper, Alliance | 4,473 | +442 | 14.2 | 4,915* |
| Hendron, SDLP | 3,612 | +1,290 | 41.3 | 4,902* |
| Gillespie, SDLP | 3,258 | +1,256 | 40.2 | 4,514 |
| Not transferred | — | 124 | 4.0 | — |

* Elected without a quota

Because three seats needed to be filled, a count with only four candidates remaining was automatically the final count. The three candidates with the largest accumulated vote totals were declared elected, although all three were short of a full quota. The lowest-ranking winner, Hugh Smyth, led Des Gillespie of the SDLP by 180 votes. However, with a different distribution of preferences, the SDLP supporters of Pascal O'Hare could have elected two SDLP men on the eighth count, rather than one. If 201 of the 442 votes transferred to Cooper had gone to O'Hare's SDLP running mate, Des Gillespie, then he rather than Bob Cooper would have taken the seat. Alternatively, if 182 of the 1,290 votes transferred to Joe Hendron, SDLP, had gone to Des Gillespie instead, then the SDLP would have taken two seats and Bob Cooper the third; Hugh Smyth, the independent Loyalist, would have been the odd man out.

The examination of vote transfers from the West Belfast count is a reminder that any electoral system, whatever its creators' aspirations to logic, can produce empirical curiosities like the result analyzed above. This affects candidates of the same party who are jockeying with each other for preferences, as well as the aggregate distribution of seats in relation to votes. Yet, taking the Province as a whole, the transfers of votes present a picture of voting regularities. For example, the West Belfast vote emphasizes the importance of party loyalties and the refusal of all but a handful of individuals to cast votes across the sectarian divide.

## Table A-1
## SOURCES OF VOTE TRANSFERS, NORTHERN IRELAND CONVENTION ELECTION

| Source | Percentage of Transfer Vote Received by Each Party, According to Source | | | | | | Not Transferred |
|---|---|---|---|---|---|---|---|
| | Loyalist | UPNI | Alliance | NILP | SDLP | Republican Clubs | |
| Loyalists | 87.7 | 30.0 | 7.3 | 52.9 | 0.6 | 0.4 | 17.3 |
| UPNI | 8.1 | 33.7 | 16.9 | 16.6 | 2.1 | 1.1 | 10.4 |
| Alliance | 2.9 | 31.0 | 38.7 | 14.0 | 17.1 | 5.8 | 27.8 |
| NILP | 0.7 | 3.5 | 5.4 | 15.9 | 0.8 | — | 2.4 |
| SDLP | 0.3 | 1.2 | 28.6 | 0.5 | 67.7 | 14.3 | 17.8 |
| Republican Clubs | 0.2 | 0.5 | 3.1 | — | 11.7 | 78.4 | 24.4 |
| | 100% | 100% | 100% | 100% | 100% | 100% | 100% |
| Total of transferred votes received | 118,596 | 23,924 | 32,874 | 2,239 | 32,732 | 4,458 | 25,441 |

Note: Totals may not add due to rounding.
Source: McAllister, *The 1975 Northern Ireland Convention Election,* p .19.

## Table A-2

### DISTRIBUTION OF VOTE TRANSFERS, NORTHERN IRELAND CONVENTION ELECTION

| Donor | How the Percentage of Donor's Vote Transferred | | | | | | Not Trans-ferred | Total Percent | Total Votes Distrib-uted |
|---|---|---|---|---|---|---|---|---|---|
| | Loyalist | UPNI | Alliance | NILP | SDLP | Republican Clubs | | | |
| Loyalists | 87.1 | 6.0 | 2.0 | 1.0 | 0.2 | — | 3.7 | 100 | 119,418 |
| UPNI | 35.7 | 29.8 | 20.5 | 1.4 | 2.6 | 0.2 | 9.9 | 100 | 27,013 |
| Alliance | 9.3 | 20.2 | 34.5 | 0.9 | 15.2 | 0.7 | 19.2 | 100 | 36,805 |
| NILP | 18.7 | 17.9 | 37.8 | 7.6 | 5.3 | — | 12.8 | 100 | 4,709 |
| SDLP | 1.1 | 0.8 | 25.1 | — | 59.0 | 1.7 | 12.1 | 100 | 37,534 |
| Republican Clubs | 1.4 | 0.8 | 6.9 | — | 25.8 | 23.5 | 41.7 | 100 | 14,872 |

**Note:** Totals may not add due to rounding.
**Source:** McAllister, *The 1975 Northern Ireland Convention Election*, p .19.

# APPENDIX B
## A Note on Readings

Understanding Northern Ireland politics is no easy task, whether one observes from a distance or from close at hand. While history cannot predict day-to-day developments, it may nonetheless help one understand tomorrow's events, for the Troubles that now beset Northern Ireland are often echoes of the past. One reason for this is that present disputes often divide people on exactly the same lines on which people divided decades or centuries ago. For example, Protestants in Londonderry witnessing the Catholic Bogside rising in 1969 felt fears like their ancestors in Londonderry more than a quarter of a millenium before. At the same time, Catholics in streets off the Falls Road in Belfast feared an invasion of Protestant attackers, unharried by police, similar to those invasions that their forefathers had experienced in the century and a half since Belfast became a populous city.

There is no such thing as a good *short* history of Ireland, nor will one find an account everywhere accepted as unbiased. The readings selected here are recommended as a starting point for inquiry. Most have footnotes or bibliographies giving further guidance. Moreover, the footnotes to this study provide guidance to books relevant to special topics, such as Ulster-American ties.

Readers seeking to learn first things first might begin, for the North, with T. W. Moody, *The Ulster Question, 1603–1973* (Cork: Mercier Press, 1974). General information about the Republic can be found in Oliver MacDonagh's *Ireland* (Englewood Cliffs, N.J.: Prentice-Hall, 1968). Relevant ground is covered in greater detail in J. C. Beckett, *The Making of Modern Ireland, 1603–1923* (London: Faber, 1966), F. S. L. Lyon, *Ireland since the Famine* (London: Weidenfeld & Nicolson, 1971), and Robert Kee, *The Green Flag: A History of*

*Irish Nationalism* (London: Weidenfeld & Nicolson, 1972). The relationship between England and Ireland is surveyed, with a wealth of insights from all over Europe, by Nicholas Mansergh, *The Irish Question, 1840–1921* (London: Allen and Unwin, 1965). A committed Ulster Unionist, T. E. Utley, brings the story up to date in *Lessons of Ulster* (London: Dent, 1975). L. P. Curtis, Jr., has produced two books, one primarily in prose, *Anglo-Saxons and Celts: A Study of Anti-Irish Prejudice in Victorian England* (distributed by the New York University Press for the Conference on British Studies, 1968), and one with illustrations, *Apes and Angels: The Irishman in Victorian Caricature* (Washington, D. C.: Smithsonian Institution, and Newton Abbott, Devon: David and Charles, 1971). Readers who think it odd to relate political views to religion will find historical precedent in E. R. Norman, ed., *Anti-Catholicism in Victorian England* (London: Allen & Unwin, 1968) and Ray Billington, *The Protestant Crusade, 1800–1860* (New York: Macmillan, 1938). J. H. Whyte, *Church and State in Modern Ireland, 1923–1970* (Dublin and London: Gill and Macmillan, 1971) provides a dispassionate account of a contentious subject. For an examination of the much neglected subject of national differences within the United Kingdom, see Richard Rose, *The United Kingdom as a Multi-National State*, conveniently reprinted in the third edition of Richard Rose, ed., *Studies in British Politics* (London: Macmillan, 1976).

For an account of conditions in Northern Ireland before the Troubles broke out in 1968–69, see Denis P. Barritt and C. F. Carter, *The Northern Ireland Problem* (London: Oxford University Press, 1962). Rosemary Harris's study, *Prejudice and Tolerance in Ulster* (Manchester: University Press, 1972) gives an anthropological account of village life, and Ian Budge and Cornelius O'Leary study city life in *Belfast—Approach to Crisis: A Study of Belfast Politics, 1613–1970* (London: Macmillan, 1973). An institutional description of forms of government can be found in periodic editions of the *Ulster Yearbook* (Belfast: Her Majesty's Stationery Office). Much of the pith of constitutional interpretation is contained in Harry Calvert, *Constitutional Law in Northern Ireland* (London: Stevens & Sons, 1968.) A. T. Q. Stewart's *The Ulster Crisis* (London: Faber, 1967) gives a full account of the Ulster Protestant threat to rebel against Britain prior to the First World War. J. Bowyer Bell's *The Secret Army* (London: Blond, 1970) is the definitive history of the IRA up to the time the Troubles started again in Ulster. The author's own *Governing without Consensus* (London: Faber, and Boston: Beacon Press, 1971) contains a lengthy historical section, as well as survey data from 1968. Robert Fisk in *The Point of No Return: The Strike which Broke the British in Ulster* (London: Deutsch, 1975), provides an informed, thorough, and fair-minded account of the events of May 1974.

The clearest factual account of the Troubles, with additional bibliography, is contained in the successive volumes of Richard Deutsch and Vivien Magowan, *Northern Ireland: A Chronology of Events*, vol. 1, 1968–71; vol. 2, 1972–73; vol. 3, 1974 (Belfast: Blackstaff Press). The files of *Fortnight*, a journal of opinion and comment, published at 7 Lower Crescent, Belfast, since 25 September 1970, bring the chronology up to date as well as providing interpretations from a variety of viewpoints. Among the three daily newspapers in the Province, the *Belfast Telegraph* presents news intended to be accepted as factual by both Protestant and Catholic readers; the Belfast *News-Letter* has an almost exclusively Protestant readership and the *Irish News* an almost exclusively Catholic readership. The *Irish Times*, published in Dublin, provides extensive reporting of political events in Northern Ireland, as well as giving Southern Irish views.

The chronicles by Deutsch and Magowan provide citations to British and Northern Ireland government White Papers concerning the Troubles, as well as pinpointing dates when press coverage of ad hoc events is extensive. Bibliographies of the literature of the Troubles include Richard Rose, "Ulster Politics: A Select Bibliography of Political Discord," *Political Studies*, vol. 20, no. 2 (1972), and J. Bowyer Bell, "The Chroniclers of Violence in Northern Ireland: The First Wave Interpreted," *Review of Politics*, vol. 34, no. 2 (1972) and "The Chroniclers Revisited: The Analysis of Tragedy," ibid., vol. 36 (1974). *A Register of Research into the Irish Conflict*, edited by John P. Darby (1972) for the now defunct Northern Ireland Community Relations Commission, gives a detailed list of scholars promising publication. T. W. Moody, ed., *Irish Historiography, 1936–70* (Dublin: Irish Committee of Historical Sciences, 1971) covers modern work by scholars concerned with all parts of the island.

The foregoing reading list may seem daunting, but the Troubles are more than three centuries old and still going strong. Even within the apparently simplifying contours of confrontation politics, there are important internal divisions. Anyone who wishes to begin to comprehend the Troubles of Northern Ireland must know a lot; a little learning can be a very dangerous thing.

# RECENT STUDIES IN FOREIGN AFFAIRS

**Northern Ireland: Time of Choice** by Richard Rose addresses Northern Ireland's most serious problem—the absence of a civil government, with or without consensus. According to Rose, Northern Ireland lacks two of the basic attributes of the modern state: a constitution and a security organization with an effective claim to a monopoly of force. In most countries where elections are held, they decide who governs; but in Northern Ireland, elections are about how the country should be governed or whether it should be governed at all. In an attempt to resolve this problem, in May 1975 the British government sponsored an election in Northern Ireland of a constitutional convention to recommend how that troubled land should be governed henceforth. Rose describes the background which resulted in direct British rule, the parties to the dispute, the ballot, the many factors leading to deadlock in the Northern Ireland Constitutional Convention, and the choices for the future of Northern Ireland.

Richard Rose, a native-born American, is professor of politics at the University of Strathclyde, Glasgow, Scotland, and has been studying Northern Ireland politics since 1965. Among his books are *Politics in England, Governing without Consensus,* and *The Problem of Party Government.* He is also a contributor to a recent AEI study, *Britain at the Polls,* covers British general elections for the *Times* (London), and appears frequently on British television as a commentator on current affairs.

**$3.75**

American Enterprise Institute for Public Policy Research
1150 Seventeenth Street, N.W., Washington, D. C. 20036